MW01269036

Understanding the Human Being
Selected writings of Rudolf Steiner

Selected and edited by

Richard Seddon

Rudolf Steiner Press
Bristol

© 1993 Rudolf Steiner Press
for the Anthroposophical Society in Great Britain

All rights reserved. No part of this publication may be
reproduced, stored in a retrieval system, or transmitted in
any form or by any means, electronic, mechanical, photo-
copying, recording or otherwise, without permission
of the copyright holder.

Published by Rudolf Steiner Press,
P.O. Box 955, Bristol BS99 5QN

First published 1988 by Crucible as
Rudolf Steiner - Essential Readings

ISBN 1 85584 005 7

Produced by The Cromwell Press, Melksham

CONTENTS

EDITOR'S FOREWORD

The work of Rudolf Steiner (1861-1925) has been strangely neglected, probably because it challenges many of the fundamental thoughts upon which modern civilization — now so often visibly destructive both of human values and of the environment — is based. Nevertheless the number of people finding that this work provides a vitalizing force, not only for their personal life but also for their professional work in many a different field, steadily increases.

Steiner had supersensible experiences from the age of eight, and a scientific education in Wiener Neustadt and Vienna. This enabled him from his youth to hold together both poles of life in a unique way. He described the results of his spiritual researches in clear thoughts that everyday intelligence, if sufficiently unprejudiced, can grasp step-by-step as in any science; and he followed a rigorous path of self-development, which he characterized in a way that can be followed by anyone prepared to make the necessary systematic effort. His early work laid a firm philosophical foundation, and from 1902 onwards periods of about seven years bore in succession the predominant character of the presentation of esoteric truths (culminating in deep insights into the nature of Christ), the revitalization of artistic life out of spiritual sources, and the reordering of education and the social life. In many fields he planted seeds now beginning to unfold.

It has been doubted whether an anthology of such a wide-ranging life's work is feasible, or indeed even desirable. Each of his books or lecture courses can be recognized as an artistic and living whole; to anthologize is to take a bone from one organism, a muscle from another — the result cannot possibly reflect the living quality of the originals! Moreover there are some 35 written volumes and 4500 lectures in transcipt from which to select, most now published in German and well over half available in English. The choice from such a wealth cannot but be influenced by the predilections of an editor, however hard he tries to present an objective selection. Steiner himself provided a comprehensive (but deliberately not easy) introduction to his own work in his book *Occult Science: An Outline*.

Nevertheless it seems important that Steiner's work should not be unrepresented in a series containing the thoughts of outstanding spiritual leaders. This selection is made in the light of his perceptive remark that the English are less interested in explanations than in spiritual facts. Preference has been given to the written works and the hundred or so lectures he gave in England, so far as subject-matter allows. Readers should not be deterred by the rather terse definitions which have to be given at the beginning of Chapter 2; these will become more meaningful in the discursive sections that follow.

It needs to be remembered that the transcripts of lectures were not edited by Steiner, and that translations cannot convey the precise nuances implicit in another language, although published translations have been revised to give some consistency of style. (The word 'man' is used throughout in its primary sense, transcending any distinction between female and male.) Moreover, because of the many facets of Steiner's thought, the editor has not hesitated for the present purpose to abridge where necessary, with the risk of clouding the original sequence of thought, rather than to omit a topic altogether. Footnotes are those of the editor unless otherwise stated. Italics are those of the author in written works, but of the editor in spoken lectures.

Anthroposophy, as Steiner called the impulse he gave, means wisdom concerning the higher self of man. It is primarily a path of knowledge, a way of knowing, rather than a teaching; but the first step on this path is the study of spiritual facts. Its view of the world, as distinct from that of most scientists, is man-centred and holistic. Man's divine origin, his necessary oblivion of this in order to become a free individuality, and his struggle to attain full spiritual stature as Man through working on earth with the forces brought by Christ (the full extent of which will only become apparent in the future) — these form the central themes of the present volume.

The spirit is here seen as the creative element in evolution. Spiritual movements may consequently be evaluated by the words 'By their fruits ye shall know them'. The Appendix therefore includes for each chapter not only the sources from which the extracts are taken and suggestions for further reading, but also particulars of some of the main practical applications of Steiner's work in Britain today; equivalents may be found in many other countries, especially those of central Europe.

Particular thanks are due to my wife Mary for her help in many ways, but especially in revising the translations and in proofreading; to members of the Council of the Anthroposophical Society in Great Britain for permission to use copyright material, and for their encouragement; and to other friends who have helped in various ways.

Richard Seddon
Ross-on-Wye
Michaelmas 1987

1

INTRODUCTORY

1. VENERATION FOR TRUTH

There slumber in *every* human being faculties by means of which he can acquire for himself knowledge of higher worlds. Mystics, gnostics, theosophists always spoke of a world of soul and spirit, which for them is just as actual as the world we see with our physical eyes and touch with our physical hands. At every moment the listener may say to himself: that of which they speak, I too can experience, if I develop within myself certain forces which today still slumber within me. There is only one question — how one has to start to develop in oneself such faculties. For this purpose, only those can give guidance who already possess such powers within themselves. As long as the human race has existed, there has always been a method of training, through which individuals possessing these higher faculties gave guidance to others who were in search of them. Such a training is called *esoteric* training, and the instruction received there is called esoteric training or spiritual science. . .

There is, in truth, no difference between esoteric knowledge and all the rest of man's knowledge and proficiency. This esoteric knowledge is no more of a secret for the average person than writing is a secret for those who have never learnt. And just as all can learn to write who choose the correct methods, so too can all who seek the corresponding ways become esoteric students, and even teachers. . .

One must begin with a certain fundamental attitude of soul. The spiritual investigator calls this fundamental attitude the *path of veneration*, of devotion for truth and knowledge. . . If we do not develop within ourselves this deeply-rooted feeling that there is something higher than ourselves, we shall never find within us the strength to evolve to something higher. The initiate has only acquired the strength to lift his head to the heights of knowledge by guiding his heart to the depths of veneration and devotion. The heights of the spirit can only be climbed by passing through the portal of humility. You can only acquire right knowledge when you have learnt to esteem it . . .

In our time, it is especially important that full attention be paid to this point. Our civilization tends more towards criticism, judgement and condemnation, and less towards devotion and selfless veneration. Our children already criticize far more than they revere with devotion. But every criticism, every adverse judgement, disperses the forces of the soul for higher knowledge, in the same degree that all veneration and reverence develops them . . . It must be emphasized that higher knowledge is *not* concerned with the veneration of persons, but with the veneration of *truth* and *knowledge* . . .

Whoever seeks higher knowledge must create it in himself. He must himself instil it into his soul. It cannot be done by study; it can only be done through life. Whoever, therefore, wishes to become a student of higher knowledge must assiduously cultivate this inner mood of devotion. Everywhere in his environment and in his experience he must seek that which can evoke in him admiration and respect. If I meet a man and blame him for his weakness, I rob myself of power to attain higher knowledge; but if I try to enter lovingly into his merits, I gather such power . . .

Every moment that we set ourselves to discover in our consciousness whatever remains in it of adverse, disparaging and critical judgement of the world and of life brings us nearer to higher knowledge. And we rise rapidly, if only we fill our consciousness in such moments with thoughts evoking in us admiration, respect and veneration for the world and for life. It is well known to those experienced in these matters that, in every such moment, forces are awakened in us which otherwise remain dormant. *In this way*, the spiritual eyes of man are opened. He thus begins to see around him things which he could not have seen before. He begins to understand that hitherto he had only seen a part of the world around him. A person standing in front of him now presents a quite different form than before. Of course, this rule of life alone will not yet enable him to see, for instance, what is described as the human aura, for which a still higher training is necessary. But he can rise to this higher training if he has previously undergone a *rigorous* training in devotion . . .

It is not easy at first for anyone to believe that feelings like reverence, respect and so on have anything to do with cognition. This is due to the fact that we are inclined to set cognition aside as a faculty by itself, that stands in no relation to what otherwise happens in the soul. But in so thinking, we do not bear in mind that it is the *soul* which exercises the faculty of cognition; and feelings are for the soul what food is for the body. If we give the body stones in place of bread, its activity will cease. It is similar with the soul. For it, veneration, homage, devotion, are as nutritive forces making it healthy and strong, especially strong for the activity of cognition. Disrespect, antipathy, underestimation of what deserves recognition, exert a paralysing and withering effect on this faculty of cognition . . .

Why does the seeking soul of man
Strive towards knowledge of higher worlds?
Because each look born of the soul
Into the world of the senses
Becomes a question, fraught with longing,
As to the being of spirit.

2. THREE KINDS OF EXPERIENCE

The following words of Goethe show, in a beautiful manner, the starting-point of one of the ways by which the nature of man can be known.

'As soon as a person becomes aware of the objects around him, he considers them in relation to himself, and rightly so, for his whole fate depends on whether they please or displease him, attract or repel, help or harm him. This quite natural way of looking at or judging things appears to be as easy as it is necessary. Nevertheless a person is exposed through it to a thousand errors which often make him ashamed and embitter his life. A far more difficult task is undertaken by those whose keen desire for knowledge urges them to strive to observe the objects of nature *in themselves* and in their relations to each other; for they soon feel the lack of the test which helped them when they, as men, regarded the objects in reference to themselves personally. They lack the test of pleasure and displeasure, attraction and repulsion, usefulness and harmfulness. This they must renounce entirely. They ought as dispassionate and, so to speak, divine beings, to seek and examine what is, and not what gratifies. Thus the true botanist should not be moved either by the beauty or by the usefulness of the plants. He has to study their formation and their relation to the rest of the vegetable kingdom; and just as they are one and all enticed forth and shone upon by the sun, so should he, with an equable, quiet glance, look at and survey them all and obtain the standard for this knowledge, the data for his deductions, not out of himself, but from within the circle of the things which he observes.'

The thought thus expressed by Goethe directs man's attention to three aspects. First, the objects concerning which information continually flows to him through the doors of his senses, the objects which he touches, smells, tastes, hears and sees. Second, the impressions which these make on him, thus characterizing themselves as his pleasure and displeasure, what he desires or abhors, so that he finds the one sympathetic, the other antipathetic; the one useful, the other harmful. Third, the knowledge which he, as 'a so-to-speak divine being' acquires concerning the objects — that is, the secrets of their activities and their existence which unveil themselves to him.

These three regions are distinctly separate in human life. And we thereby become aware that we are interwoven with the world in a threefold way. The first way is something that we find present, which we accept as a given fact. Through the second way we make the world into our own affair, into something that has a meaning for ourselves. The third way we regard as a goal towards which we have unceasingly to strive. . . We should not, for the time being, read anything into this fact, but merely take it as it stands. There follows from it that man has three sides to his nature. This and nothing else will for the present be indicated here by the three words body, soul and spirit. Whoever connects any preconceived opinions, or even hypotheses, with these three words will necessarily misunderstand the following explanations. By *body* is here meant that through which the things in our environment reveal themselves to us. By the word *soul* is signified that by which we link the things to our own being, through which we experience pleasure and displeasure, desire and aversion, joy and sorrow, in relation to them. By *spirit* is meant that which becomes manifest in us when, as Goethe expressed it, we look at things as a 'so-to-speak divine being'. In this sense the human being consists of body, soul and spirit.

Through his body man is able to place himself, for the moment, in connection with things; through his soul he retains in himself the impressions which they make on him; through his spirit there reveals itself to him what the things retain for themselves. Only when we observe man in these three aspects can we hope to gain an explanation of his whole being, for these three aspects show man to be related in a threefold way to the rest of the world.

Through his body he is related to the objects which present themselves to his senses from without. The materials from the outer world compose this body of his; and the forces of the outer world also work in it. And just as he observes the things of the outer world with his senses, so he can also observe his own bodily existence. But it is impossible to observe the soul existence in the same say. Everything in me which is bodily process can also be perceived with my bodily senses. My likes and dislikes, my joy and pain, neither I nor anyone else can perceive with bodily senses. The region of the soul is one which is inaccessible to bodily perception. The bodily existence of a man is manifest to all eyes; the soul existence he carries within himself as *his* world. Through the spirit, however, the outer world is revealed in a higher way. The mysteries of the outer world indeed unveil themselves in man's inner being, but he steps in spirit out of himself, and lets the things speak about themselves, about that which has significance not for him but for *them*. Man looks up at the starry heavens; the delight his soul experiences belongs to him; the eternal laws of the stars which he comprehends in thought, in spirit, belong not to him but to the stars themselves.

Thus man is citizen of three worlds. Through his *body* he belongs to the world which he also perceives through his body; through his *soul* he constructs for himself his own world; through his *spirit* a world reveals itself to him which is exalted above both the others.

It seems evident that because of the essential differences of these three worlds we can only obtain a clear understanding of them and of man's share in them by means of three different modes of observation.

I would kindle every man from cosmic spirit,
That he become a flame
And fierily unfold in himself
The Being of his Being.

Others would take water from the cosmos
With which to quench the flames,
And to flood and drown
The whole Being within.

Oh joy, when the human flame
Blazes where it resides;
Oh bitterness, when the human thing
Becomes bound, where it might be active.

3. PREPARATION THROUGH STUDY

It is true in principle that the reader will find in the expositions of spiritual science a description of soul experiences which, if he follows them, can lead him towards the supersensible content of the world. In practice, however, this is a kind of ideal. The reader must first receive, as simple communications, a wealth of supersensible discoveries which he cannot yet experience for himself. It cannot be otherwise, and will be so in this book.* The author will be describing what he believes himself to know about the being of man, including what man undergoes in birth and death and in the body-free condition in the spiritual world; also about the evolution of the earth and of mankind. It might then seem as though he were putting forward all these alleged items of knowledge as dogmas, for which belief in authority was required. But it is not so. For in reality, whatever can be known of the supersensible world lives in the spiritual investigator as a living content of soul, and as the reader finds his way into this living content, it kindles in his soul the impulses leading towards the supersensible realities in question. The way we live in reading the descriptions of spiritual science is different from what it is when reading communications about sense-perceptible events. We simply read *about* the latter, but when we read communications of supersensible realities in the right way, we ourselves are entering into a stream of spiritual life and being. In receiving the results of research, we are receiving at the same time our own inner

*i.e. *Occult Science: An Outline*, from which this extract is taken.

path towards these results. True, to begin with, the reader will often fail to notice that this is so. For he is far too apt to conceive the entry into the spiritual world on the analogy of sensory experience. Therefore what he experiences of this world in reading of it is much too like 'mere thoughts'. Yet in the *true* receiving of it in the form of thoughts, man is already *within* the spiritual world; it only remains for him to become aware that he has been experiencing in all reality what he imagined himself to be receiving as the mere communication of thoughts.

The true character of the experience will be made fully clear to him when he proceeds to carry out in practice what is described in the later portions of this book, namely the 'path' leading to supersensible knowledge. It might easily be imagined that the reverse was the right order — the pathway should first be described. But it is not so. One who, without first turning his attention to some of the essential facts of the supersensible world, merely does 'exercises' with the idea of gaining entrance there, will find in it a vague and confusing chaos. Man finds his way into that world — to begin with, as it were, naïvely — by learning to understand its essential features. Then he can gain a clear idea of how, leaving this naïve stage behind him, he will himself attain in full consciousness to the experiences which have been related to him. Anyone who really enters into spiritual science will become convinced that this alone is the reliable way to supersensible knowledge. As to the opinion that information about the supersensible world might influence the reader by way of suggestion or mere dogma, he will perceive that this is unfounded. The contents of supersensible knowledge are experienced in a form of inner life which excludes anything in the nature of suggestion, and leaves no other possibility than to impart the knowledge to one's fellow man in the same way as any other kind of truth would be imparted, appealing only to his wide-awake and thoughtful judgement. And if, to begin with, the one who hears or reads the description does not notice how he himself is living in the spiritual world, the reason lies not in any passive or thoughtless receiving of the information but in the delicate and unwonted nature of the experience.

Therefore by studying the communications given in the first part of this book, one is enabled in the first place to participate in the knowledge of the supersensible world; thereafter, by the practical application of the procedures indicated in the second part, one can gain independent knowledge in that world.

A scientific man, entering into the spirit of this book, will find no essential contradiction between his form of science built upon the facts of the sense-perceptible world and the way the supersensible world is here investigated. Every scientist makes use of instruments and methods. He prepares his instruments by working upon the things which nature gives him. The supersensible form of knowledge also makes use of an instrument, only here the instrument is Man himself. This instrument, too, must first be prepared for the purposes of a higher kind of research. The faculties and forces with which the human instrument has been endowed by nature, without man's active co-operation, must be transformed into higher ones. Thus can a person make of himself the instrument of research into the supersensible world.

From the luminious heights of the spirit
May God's clear light ray forth
Into those human souls
Who are intent on seeking
The grace of the spirit,
The strength of the spirit,
The being of the spirit.
May He live in our hearts,
In our inmost souls,
We who feel ourselves
Gathered together here
In His name.

(For a study group in London, 1913.)

2

THE NATURE OF MAN

1. MAN'S SEVENFOLD NATURE

Let us consider the nature and being of man. When we meet someone, we first see through our sense-organs what we call the *physical body*. Man has this body in common with the whole surrounding world. And although the physical body is only a small part of what man really is, it is the only part of which ordinary science takes account. But we must go deeper. Even superficial consideration will make it clear that this physical body has very special qualities. There are plenty of other things you can see and touch; every stone is, after all, a physical body. But man can move, feel and think; he grows, takes nourishment, propagates his kind. None of this is true of a stone, but it is certainly true of plants and animals. Man has in common with the plants his capacity to nourish himself, to grow and propagate; if he were like a stone, with only a physical body, none of this would be possible. Thus he must have something which enables him to use substances and forces in such a way that they become the means of growth and so forth. This is the *etheric body*. Man has a physical body in common with the mineral kingdom and an etheric body in common with the plant and animal kingdoms. Ordinary observation can confirm that.

But there is another way to convince ourselves of the existence of the etheric body, although only those who have developed higher senses have this capacity. These higher senses are no more than a development of what is dormant in every human being. It is rather like a man born blind being operated on so that he can see; except that not everyone born blind can be successfully operated on, whereas everyone who has the necessary patience and goes through the proper training can develop the spiritual senses... Anyone who wants to know the nature of the etheric body by direct vision must be able to maintain his ordinary consciousness intact and suggest away the physical body by the strength of his own will. The gap left will not however be empty; he will see the etheric body glowing with a reddish-blue light like a phantom, but with radiance, a little darker than young peach blossom. We never see an etheric body if we suggest away a crystal, but in the case of a plant or animal we do, for it is the etheric body which is responsible for nutrition, growth and reproduction.

Man has, of course, other faculties; he can feel pleasure and pain, which the plant cannot. The initiate can discover this by his own experience, for he can identify himself with the plant. Animals feel pleasure and pain, for they have a further principle in common with man: the *astral body*. This is the seat of all that we know as desire, passion, and so on. This is again clear to straightforward observation as inner experience, but for the initiate the astral body can become an outer reality; he sees it as an egg-shaped cloud, continually mobile within, which not only surrounds the body but also permeates it. If we suggest away both physical and etheric bodies, we shall see a delicate cloud of light, inwardly full of movement. Within it, the initiate sees every desire, every impulse, as colour and form in the astral body; for example, he sees intense passion flashing like rays of lightning out of the astral body. In animals the basic colour of the astral body varies with the species; that of a lion differs from that of a lamb. Even in human beings the colour is not always the same, and if you train yourself to be sensitive to delicate nuances you will be able to recognize a man's temperament and general disposition. Nervous people have a dappled aura; the spots are not static but keep on lighting up and fading away. This is always so, and is why the aura cannot be painted.

But man is distinguished from the animal in still another way. This fourth member of man's being comes to expression in a name different from all others. I can say 'I' only of myself. In the whole of language there is no other name which cannot be applied by everyone to the same object; but a man can only say 'I' of himself. Initiates have always been aware of this. Hebrew initiates spoke of the 'inexpressible name of God', of the God who dwells in man. . . Hence the mood of wonder which passed through the listeners when the name 'Jahve' was uttered, for Jahve (or Jehovah) signifies 'I' or 'I am'. In the name which the soul uses only of itself, the God begins to speak within that individual soul. This attribute makes man superior to the animals. We must realize the tremendous significance of this word 'I'. When Jean Paul had discovered the 'I' within himself, he knew he had experienced his immortal being. Again it presents itself to the seer in a particular form. When he studies the astral body, everything appears in perpetual movement except for one small space, shaped like a somewhat elongated blue oval, at the base of the nose behind the brow. This is to be seen only in human beings, more clearly in the less civilized, mostly clearly of all at the lowest level of culture. Actually there is nothing there but an empty space: just as the empty centre of a flame appears blue when seen through the light around it, so this empty space appears blue because of the auric light streaming around it. This is the outer expression of the I or ego.

But there is a difference between a primitive and a civilized man, and also between the latter and a Francis of Assisi or a Schiller. A refinement of the moral nature produces finer colours in the aura; an increase in the power of discrimination between good and evil likewise. In the process of civilizing, the 'I' has worked on the astral body and ennobled the desires. The higher the moral and mental development of man, the more will his 'I' have worked on the astral body, and the seer can distinguish this. Whatever part of the astral body has been thus transformed by the 'I' is called *Spirit Self* (Manas), the fifth member of man's nature. A man has just so much of Spirit Self as he has created by his own efforts out of his astral body.

Man is not able to influence his etheric body directly; but in the same way that he can raise himself to a higher moral level he can also learn how to work on the etheric body. He can thus attain to mastery over it, and what he has transformed in the etheric body by his own efforts is called *Life Spirit* (Buddhi). This is the sixth member of man's nature. He then has the same temperament and habits as in his previous incarnation, because he has worked consciously on the etheric body, which is the bearer of the forces of growth and reproduction.

The highest achievement open to man on Earth is to work right down into his physical body; that is the most difficult task of all. To do so, a man must learn to control the breath and circulation, to follow consciously the activity of the nerves, and to regulate the processes underlying thought. He will then have developed in himself what we call *Spirit Man* (Atma), the seventh member of man's being.

In every human being four members are fully formed: physical body, etheric body, astral body and 'I' or ego. The fifth, Spirit Self, is only partly formed. The sixth and seventh, Life Spirit and Spirit Man, are in rudiment only. Through these seven members he can participate in the three worlds.

In the heart the loom of feeling,
In the head the light of thinking,
In the limbs the strength of will.
   Weaving of radiant light,
   Strength of the weaving,
   Light of the surging strength:
     Lo, this is Man.

2. LEVELS OF CONSCIOUSNESS

We will now consider in sequence the incarnations passed through by our planet,* realizing that these were embodiments or conditions of our earth which we have called Ancient Saturn, Ancient Sun and Ancient Moon. We must be aware that these incarnations were necessary for the development of everything living, especially man, and that man's own evolution is intimately connected with that of the Earth...

Everything in the world has evolved, even our consciousness. The consciousness that man has today he has not always possessed; it has only gradually become what it is now. We call this present consciousness 'object-consciousness' or 'waking day-consciousness'. You all know it as that which you have from morning when you awake to evening when you fall asleep. Let us be clear as to its nature. It consists in man's turning his senses towards

*For a full exposition of this remarkable concept — long known to occultism — see *Occult Science: An Outline*, Ch. 4.

the outer world and perceiving objects — that is why we call it object-consciousness. . . . What man thus perceives with his senses he reflects upon; he employs his reason to understand these different objects, and it is in these facts of sense-perception and their comprehension in the mind that present waking day-consciousness consists. Man has not always had this consciousness; it had first to develop, and he will not always have it as it is, but will ascend to higher stages.

Now with the means supplied by spiritual science we can survey seven states of consciousness, of which our present is the middle one: we can survey three preceding ones and three that follow. Many may wonder why we are just standing so nicely in the centre. This comes from the fact that other stages preceding the first are beyond our sight, others follow the seventh which are again beyond our sight, just as when you go into the fields you can see as far to the left as to the right. These seven states of consciousness will now be described.

First was a very dull deep condition of consciousness, which humanity hardly knows today. Only persons with a special mediumistic tendency can still have this consciousness today, which was once upon Ancient Saturn possessed by all men. All other states of consciousness in them have been deadened, and they appear practically lifeless. But if, from memory or even in this condition, they sketch or describe what they have experienced, they make all sorts of drawings, which, although grotesque and distorted, accord with what we call cosmic conditions. They are often entirely incorrect, but nevertheless we can recognize that such people during this lowered condition have a dull but universal consciousness; they see cosmic bodies. A consciousness that is dull like this, but nevertheless represents a universal knowledge in our cosmos, was once possessed by man on the first incarnation of our earth, and is called 'deep trance consciousness'. There are entities in our surroundings who still have such a consciousness, the minerals. If you could talk with them, they would tell you what goes on in Ancient Saturn; but this consciousness is entirely dull and insensible.

The second condition of consciousness is that of ordinary sleep. This condition is not so comprehensive, but in spite of being very dull it is clear in comparison with the first. This 'sleep-consciousness' was once the permanent state of all human beings when the earth was Ancient Sun; at that time, the human ancestor was in a continuous sleep. Even today, this state of consciousness still exists; the plants have it; they are beings who uninterruptedly sleep, and if they could speak they could tell us how things are on the Ancient Sun, for they have a Sun-consciousness.

The third condition, which is still dim and dull in relation to our day-consciousness, is that of 'picture-consciousness', and of this we have a clear idea since we experence an echo of it in our dream-filled sleep, though this is but a rudiment of what on the Ancient Moon was the consciousness of all human beings. . . The dream of present-day man *symbolizes* events both external and internal. But it was not so when this third state of consciousness was that of Moon humanity. In that time, man lived entirely in such pictures as he has in the modern dream, but they expressed realities. They signified such a reality precisely as today the colour blue signifies a reality; but at that time, colour hovered freely in space and was not resting upon objects. . . Let us suppose that one man on Ancient Moon had met another, then a freely hovering picture of form and colour would have risen up before him. Let us say an ugly one, then the man would have turned aside in order not to meet it; or a beautiful one, then he would have drawn near it. The ugly colour picture would have shown him that the other had an unsympathetic feeling towards him; the beautiful, that the other liked him. . . The pictures of colour and form denoted what was going on around him; above all, things of a soul nature and those which affected the soul, what was advantageous or harmful to it. In this way the human being orientated himself rightly with regard to things around him. . . Even today you still have this consciousness among all those animals — note this carefully — which cannot utter sounds from their inner being. There is, in fact, a far truer division of animals in esotericism than in external natural science, namely into those which can utter sounds from within and those which are dumb. It is true that one can find among certain lower creatures the power of producing sound, but this happens in a mechanical way, through friction etc., not from their inner being. . . All animals which do not utter sounds from within have such a picture-consciousness. If some lower animal, the crab for example, perceives a picture that makes a distinctly unpleasant impression, it gets out of the way; it does not see the objects, but sees the harmfulness in a repelling picture.

The fourth state of consciousness is that which all men now have. The pictures, which man formerly perceived as colour pictures floating freely in space, wrap themselves, so to speak, round the objects. One might say they are laid over them, they form the boundaries and seem to be upon the objects, whereas they formerly floated free. In consequence, they have become the expression of the form; what man earlier had within himself has come out and fastened itself on the objects, and through this he has come to his present waking day-consciousness.

Man's physical body was prepared on Saturn; on the Sun was added the etheric or life body, which interpenetrated and worked upon it. It took what the physical body had already become by itself, and worked on it further. On the Moon was added the astral body; this still further altered the form of the body. On Saturn the physical body was very simple, on the Sun it was much more complicated, for then the etheric body worked on it and made it more perfect. On the Moon the astral body was added, and on Earth the ego, which made it still more perfect... The wonderful construction of the human eye, the wonderful apparatus of the ear, all this has attained its perfection today only because it was formed out of the substance of Saturn, and the etheric body, the astral body and the ego have worked on it. So too the larynx; it was already laid down on Saturn, but man could not as yet speak... On the Sun, the sense organs were further elaborated, and all those organs were added which are primarily organs of secretion and life, which serve nutrition and growth. Then the astral body worked further during the Moon existence; the ego during the Earth existence; and thus the glands, the organs of growth and so on, matured to their present perfection. Then, on the Moon, the nervous system originated through the incorporation of the astral body. The principle, however, which enabled the human being to evolve an object-consciousness and at the same time gave him the power to send forth his pleasure and pain from within — the ego — formed in man the blood. Thus the whole universe is the builder of the sense organs; thus have all the glands, organs of reproduction and nutrition been formed by the life body; thus is the astral body the builder of the nervous system; and the ego is the incorporator of the blood...

Now let us consider the three states of consciousness which are still to come... The initiate can have them even today in anticipation. The next state known to the initiate is the so-called 'psychic-consciousness' or Imagination, in which one has both the picture-consciousness and the waking day-consciousness together. With this consciousness one sees a man in outline and in forms, as in day-waking consciousness, but one sees at the same time what lives in his soul, streaming out as coloured clouds and pictures into what is called the aura. One does not go about the world in a dreamy state like the Moon human being, but in complete self-control as a modern man of the waking consciousness. On the planet which will replace our Earth, the whole of humanity will have this psychic-consciousness or Imagination, the 'Jupiter' consciousness.

Then there is a sixth state of consciousness man will one day possess. This will unite the present day-consciousness, the psychic-consciousness known only to the initiate, and in addition all that man sleeps away today. Man will look deep, deep into the nature of beings, when he lives in this consciousness, the consciousness of Inspiration. He will not only perceive in pictures and forms of colour, he will hear the being of the other give forth sounds and tones. Each human individuality will have a certain note, and the whole will sound together in a symphony. This will be the consciousness of man when our planet will have passed into the 'Venus' condition. There he will experience the sphere-harmony which Goethe describes in his Prologue to Faust:

'The Sun-orb sings, in emulation 'mid brother-spheres, his ancient round; His path predestined through Creation he ends with steps of thunder-sound.'

When the Earth was Sun, the human being was aware in a dim way of this ringing and resounding, and on Venus he will again hear it ringing and resounding 'as of old'. To this very phrase Goethe has retained the picture.

The seventh state of consciousness is the 'spiritual consciousness' or Intuition, the very highest, when man has a universal consciousness; when he will not only see what proceeds on his own planet, but in the whole cosmos around him. It is the consciousness man had on Saturn, a kind of universal consciousness, although then quite dull, which he will have in addition to all the other states of consciousness when he will have reached 'Vulcan'.

These are the seven states of human consciousness which man must go through in his journey through the cosmos. And each incarnation of the Earth produces the conditions through which such states become possible. . . . Each planetary stage is bound up with the development of one of the seven states of human consciousness, and through what takes place on each planet the physical organs for such a state of consciousness are perfected.

3. THE EVOLUTION OF EGO-CONSCIOUSNESS

We must consider the division of the post-Atlantean period of Earth evolution* into the following epochs: first the ancient Indian; second the ancient Persian; third the Babylonian-Assyrian-Chaldean-Egyptian; fourth the Greco-Latin; and fifth the epoch in which we now live. Ours will be replaced by a sixth and that by a seventh epoch of evolution within the post-Atlantean period. We are now in the fifth of these epochs, and say to ourselves: Christianity entered into human evolution in its full profundity and significance in the fourth epoch. It has had its influence, to the extent that humanity of the fifth epoch has grasped it, and we shall now forecast prophetically what its further effect will be, so far as this is possible out of spiritual science.

The mission of Christianity was already prepared in the third epoch, to which Egyptian civilization belongs. Out of its womb, the adherents of the Old Testament directed the development of Hebrew culture in such a way that Christianity was born, as it were, out of this third epoch, coming fully into the world in the fourth epoch in the person of Christ Jesus. We may say that humanity experienced a certain spiritual influence in the third epoch of the post-Atlantean period. This worked on into the fourth epoch,

*The Atlantean was the name given to the central of the seven main periods of Earth evolution. Our post-Atlantean period has continued the downward evolution until the coming of Christ. Involution now begins. See further: *Occult Science: An Outline*, Ch. 4.

concentrating in the person of Christ Jesus, then continued on into
the fifth, our own, and from thence it will work into the sixth
epoch which will follow. Now we must clearly understand how
all this has occurred.

Let us call exactly to mind that, in the course of human evolution, the various constituent parts of the human being have
experienced their evolution. When the Atlantean Flood occurred,
the *physical body* of man was permeated by the power of the 'I am';
this means that human progress had advanced so far as to have prepared the physical instrument for the ego, or for self-consciousness.
If we were to go back into the middle of the Atlantean period, we
should find no human being in the position to develop a self-
conciousness in which it was possible for him to speak the words
'I am an I' or 'I am' out of himself. . . What was the mission of
Atlantis? It was to implant the ego in man, to imprint it upon him,
and this mission then reached beyond the Flood — described as
the Deluge — over into our age. In our post-Atlantean period,
however, a Spirit Self had gradually to enter into the human being.
After we have passed through various embodiments in our sixth
or seventh epochs, Spirit Self will have overshadowed us to a certain degree. But a longer preparation is needed for man to become
at all a fit instrument for this Spirit Self. Before that, even though
it may take thousands of years, he will first have to become a true
bearer of the 'I' or ego. He will not only have to make his physical body an instrument for the ego, but the other members of his
being as well.

In the first epoch of the post-Atlantean period, man for the first
time made his *ether body* into a bearer of the ego, just as he had
previously done with his physical body. This was the ancient Indian
civilization.

If we now wish to consider the further evolution of these cultural epochs in relation to men, we have to consider the soul not
merely superficially as the astral body, but we must proceed more
accurately, and take as a basis the membering which you find in
my book *Theosophy*, or *Occult Science*. There we distinguish the soul
body from the sentient soul, the intellectual soul, and the consciousness soul. Then we have the higher members, Spirit Self, Life
Spirit and Spirit Man. The fourth member, which we summarized
under the name 'ego', we must divide, because in human evolu-

tion it is thus divided.

What was developed during the Ancient Persian epoch is actually the soul body or *sentient body*. It is the bearer of the active human forces; therefore the transition from the Indian to the Persian epoch consisted in passing over from a state of inactivity to one of activity in the material world. The movement of the hands and everything that was connected with them, the transition to work, is what characterized this epoch. (To a much greater degree than is supposed, the inhabitants of Ancient India were disinclined to bestir their hands, but were much more inclined to lift themselves in contemplation above material existence into higher worlds. They had to penetrate deeply into their inner being when they wished to call to memory earlier conditions. Thus Indian yoga, for example, consisted in general in giving special care and cultivation to the etheric body.)

Now let us proceed further. In the culture of the Assyrian-Babylonian-Chaldean-Egyptian epoch, the ego mounts into the *sentient soul*. The sentient soul is the means by which the sensing human being directs himself outwards, by which the perceiving human being activates his eyes and other senses and becomes aware of the ruling spirit in outer nature. Consequently in that epoch the eyes were directed toward the material things spread out in space, towards the stars and their courses. What was spread out in space externally acted upon the sentient soul. Very little then existed as yet of what can be called an inner, personal and intellectual culture. We today can no longer really imagine what constituted the Egyptian wisdom of that epoch. It was, in fact, not at all a matter of thinking, of speculation, as was the case later on; but when man turned his glance outwards, he received the law as he read externally with his senses; it was a reading of the laws, a science of perception, of feeling, not a science of concepts.

History points out that the real founder of logic was Aristotle. If there had previously been a logic, a science of thought, it would have been possible to inscribe it in a book. A logic, that is a process of reflection in the ego, in which concepts are separated and united within the ego, where one forms judgements logically and does not gather them from the things themselves, first appeared in the fourth cultural epoch. Therefore we call this fourth epoch that of the *intellectual* soul.

We ourselves are now in the epoch of the appearance of the ego in the *consciousness* soul. The ego first entered the consciousness soul about the middle of the Middle Ages. This can be very easily proved historically, and light could be thrown into every corner. At that time a very definite concept was implanted in mankind, that of indivdual freedom, of individual ego-capacity. If you consider the early part of the Middle Ages, you will still find everywhere that the value of the individual depended in a certain sense on his position in the community. A person inherited his standing, his rank and position, from his father and his kinsmen, and in accordance with these impersonal things, which are not consciously connected with the ego, he acted and worked in the world. Only later, when commerce expanded and inventions and modern discoveries were made, did ego-consciousness begin to extend, and we can see arising everywhere in the European world the extenal reflection of this consciousness soul, in very definite forms of municipal government, municipal constitutions, etc. What in the Middle Ages was called the 'free city' is the external counterpart of this breathing of the ego-conscious soul through humanity. And if we now allow our glance to sweep into the future, we may say: we are now about to develop this personal consciousness within the consciousness soul. All the demands of the modern age are nothing but the demands of the consciousness soul which mankind is unconsciously expressing.

But when we look still further into the future, we see spiritually something else. The human being rises in the next cultural epoch to *Spirit Self*. That will be a time when men will possess a common wisdom in a very much greater degree than at present; they will be as it were immersed in a common wisdom. This will be the beginning of the feeling that the innermost kernel of the human being is the most universally valid. What is looked upon as the possession of the individual in the present sense of the word is not yet so on a higher plane. At present there is a notion, closely linked with the individuality, with the human personality, that human beings must contend with one another, must have different opinions. Men say that if we could not have different opinions, we would not be independent beings. Just because they wish to be independent, they must hold different opinions. That, however, is an inferior point of view. Men will be most peaceful and harmonious when as separate persons they become most individualized. As long as men are not yet overshadowed by Spirit Self there will be opinions which differ from each other. These opinions are not yet experienced in the true innermost part of their being. At present there are only a few forerunners of things experienced in the depths of the soul, and these are the mathematical and geometrical truths. These cannot be put to the vote. . .

It will be Spirit Self culture when more and more the sources of truth are experienced within the strengthened human individuality, within the personality, and when at the same time there is an agreement between what different people experience as higher reality, just as now there is agreement between what they experience as the truths of mathematics. . . For those who see more deeply into the nature of things, it is quite impossible to disagree about their higher nature; there is only one possibility for those who disagree: that of developing themselves to perceive more deeply. Then truth discovered in one soul will coincide exactly with that in another, and there will be no more strife. That is the guarantee for true peace and true brotherhood; because there is but *one* truth, and this truth has something to do with the spiritual sun. Just think how orderly is plant growth: each plant grows towards the sun, and there is only a single sun. Thus in the course of the sixth cultural epoch, when Spirit Self draws into human beings, a spiritual sun will actually be present, toward which all men will incline, and in which they will be in agreement. That is the great perspective which we have in prospect for the sixth epoch.

Then in the seventh epoch, *Life Spirit* will, in a certain way, enter into our evolution. This is the far distant future toward which, only divining, we can turn our glance. But we now see clearly that the sixth epoch, which will come, will be very important, because it will bring peace and brotherhood through a common wisdom. . .

Creature ranks with creature in the widths of space,
Creature follows creature in the rounds of time.
If you linger in the widths of space, in rounds of time,
You are, O Man, in realms that pass away.
Yet mightily your soul rises above them
When you divine or knowingly behold the eternal
Beyond the widths of space, beyond the course of time.

4. INNER EXPERIENCES OF SLEEP

Whereas during waking life man is related to the external earthly substances, when he passes over into sleep he comes into a certain connection with the whole cosmos. It is not that his astral body assumes every night the vastness of the cosmos — that would be an exaggeration; nevertheless every night man grows out into the cosmos. . . Whilst we sleep the starry heavens become our world, just as the Earth is our world while we are awake.

Now we can distinguish different spheres through which we pass between falling asleep and waking. In the first sphere the ego and astral body — the soul as it exists during sleep — feel united with the movements of the world of the planets. . . It is not that we receive into us every night the entire planetary movement; we carry within us a little picture in which the actual movements of the planets are reproduced. And this picture is different for each person. Each of us, on falling asleep, experiences first the planetary movements, all that happens between the planets as they move out there in the wide spaces of the universe; we experience it all inwardly in the astral body as a sort of planetary globe.

Do not say, 'How does this concern me, for I do not perceive it?' You do not see it with your eyes or hear it with your ears; but the moment you go to sleep, the part of your astral body which belongs in waking life to your heart actually becomes for you what we may call a *heart-eye*, and this becomes an organ of vision for what takes place in this way; it really perceives what man experiences there, though for mankind of today the perception is very dim. It works in such a way that very soon after you have fallen asleep the heart-eye looks back at what has been left lying in bed, your ego and astral body look back with the heart-eye at your physical and etheric bodies. And the picture in your body of the planetary movements that you now experience rays back to you from your own etheric body, and you have a reflection of it.

Man is so constituted today that as soon as he wakes up he forgets the dim consciousness that he had at night by means of this heart-eye. At most a dim consciousness echoes in such dreams as have still in their inner mobility something of the planetary movement. Into these dreams come pictures from real life, because

the astral body dives down into the ether body, which preserves
for us the memories of life. It might happen that you wake up,
having passed again on your return through the sphere of planetary
movements and having experienced, for example, a particular
relationship between Jupiter and Venus, because this was intimately
connected with your destiny. If you could bring the experience
of this relationship back into your ordinary life of day, it would
shed considerable light on your human capacities; for these faculties
derive not from the earth but from the cosmos — according to
your connection with the cosmos so are your gifts and talents, your
goodness, or at any rate your inclination to good or evil. You
would see what Jupiter and Venus were saying to one another,
which you had perceived with your heart-eye or heart-ear, for one
cannot distinguish so exactly between them. Since, however, all
this is only dimly perceived, it is forgotten; but the mutual
relationship between Jupiter and Venus still produces a
corresponding movement within your astral body. Now there
mingles with it some experience you had long ago, let us say at
noon one day in Oxford or Manchester; these pictures mingle with
the cosmic experience. Thus the pictures given us in dreams have
a certain significance, yet they are not the essential part of the
dream; they are like a garment that weaves around the cosmic
experience.

Now this whole heart experience is combined with a certain
anxiety; in almost everyone it is intermingled with a more or less
intense feeling of anxiety of a spiritual nature, particularly when
the cosmic experience sounds back, shines back, from the ether-
body to the soul. Suppose due to the relationship of Jupiter and
Venus one ray, which tells much to your heart-perception, comes
back from your forehead, while a second comes from below the
heart and mingles its tone and light with the first; this will give
rise to the feeling of anxiety. Every human soul that is not completely hardened actually says to itself in sleep: The cosmic mist
has received me into itself. It is really as if one becomes as thin
as the cosmic mist and floats as a cloud of mist in the Mist of
Worlds. Such is the immediate experience after falling asleep. And
then out of this anxiety and the experience of ourself, as a waft
of mist within the Mist of Worlds, another mood develops in the
soul, a mood of devotion to the divine that pervades the universe.

The fundamental feelings that come towards us in the first sphere after falling asleep are: I am in the Mist of Worlds — I would fain rest in the womb of the Godhead, that I be safe from dissolving in the Mist of Worlds.

This is something which the heart-perception must carry over in the morning when the soul dives down again into the physical and etheric bodies. For if this experience were not brought over into life, then the substances which we take as nourishment next day would retain within us their own completely earthly character, and throw our whole organism into disorder; even if we go hungry, substances are continually being consumed from our own body. Sleep has in fact immense and significant meaning for the waking condition. And we can only be grateful that in this epoch of evolution it is not left to man himself to ensure that the divine is carried over into waking life. For men of today would scarcely be able to muster the strength to bring these influences over in full consciousness from the other side of existence to this side.

Then man comes into the next sphere, though he does not leave the first — it remains for his heart-perception. This next sphere, which is much more complicated, is perceived by that part of the astral body which belongs in waking life to the solar plexus and the whole limb-organization. In this next sphere man feels in his astral body the forces that come from the constellations of the zodiac; forces come in one form direct from the zodiac and in another form through the Earth, for it makes a great difference whether a particular constellation is above or below the earth. Thus man perceives with what I might now call a sun-perception, because it is concerned as an organ of perception with that part of the astral body that is associated with the solar plexus and limbs — I would like to call it his 'sun-eye'. Through this he becomes aware of his whole relationship to the zodiac and the planetary movement. Thus the picture widens, and man grows further into the cosmic picture. Again he receives that which is reflected from his physical and etheric bodies, on which he turns back his gaze. Thus every night it is given to that part of man which goes out of his body to come into a relationship to the whole cosmos, the planetary movement and the constellations.

In this experience with the fixed stars, which may come half an hour after falling asleep or rather later, but in many people quite soon, man experiences himself within all twelve constellations, and the experiences he encounters with these constellations are exceedingly complicated. You might have travelled far and wide and visited the most important regions of the earth, and yet not have had so many experiences as your sun-eye affords every night in relation to one single constellation. For the men of an older time, who still had strong powers of dreamlike clairvoyance and perceived in dream-consciousness much of what has been described, the experiences of sleep were less bewildering. Today a man can scarcely attain to any degree of clarity with his sun-eye — and he needs to do so, even if by day he has forgotten it — concerning what he has experienced of this complicated twelve-fold experience during the night, unless he has received with heart-understanding all that Christ willed the Earth to become through the mystery of Golgotha. To have once felt what it means for the life of the Earth that Christ has gone through the mystery of Golgotha, to have formed thoughts about Christ in our ordinary waking life, brings to the astral body by way of the physical and etheric bodies a certain colouring or tincture which brings it about that Christ become our guide through the zodiac during sleep. Man actually feels once again: What if I lose myself in the multitude of stars and all that happens there? But if he can look back on thoughts, feelings and impulses of will that he has directed in waking life to Christ, then Christ becomes for him a guide, bringing order into the bewildering events of this sphere.

So we must actually say that only when we turn our attention to the other side of life can we appreciate the full significance of Christ for the earthly life of mankind since the mystery of Golgotha; and practically no one can otherwise really understand what Christ has yet to become for earthly life. These things, which not many people yet pass through, are wrongly interpreted. People today who have not come in touch with the Christ Event bring these night experiences into waking day-consciousness in a disordered way; we first understand them when we know what has been described. In fact when we have passed during sleep through the mist-condition, we face a world that bewilders us. Here Christ appears before us as a spiritual Sun and becomes our guide, so that the confusion resolves into a kind of harmonious understanding.

That is important, because the moment we enter this sphere, in which we have a whirling interweaving of the constellations of the zodiac and the movements of the planets, our destiny actually appears before our sun-eye. Everyone perceives his destiny, but in a condition of sleep; in the waking condition only the after-echo of this perception creeps into the feelings. Much of the condition which men striving for self-knowledge can encounter within themselves is the after-echo of this experience, where Christ comes forward as their guide and leads them on from Aries through Taurus and Gemini etc., making the universe clear to them during the night, so that they gain strength for the life of day. For what we experience in this sphere is nothing less than the fact that Christ becomes our leader through the confusing happenings of the zodiac; that as leader He stands there and guides us from constellation to constellation, so that we can receive into ourself in an ordered way the forces we need for waking life.

5. TWO TYPES OF DREAM

Let us now consider dream life as it appears to us. We can distinguish two quite different kinds. The first conjures pictures of outer experiences before our soul. Years ago, or perhaps a few days, we experienced this or that in a definite way; the dream conjures out of sleep a picture more or less similar — usually dissimilar — to the outer experience. If we discover any connection between this dream-picture and the outer experience, we are at once struck by the transformation that the latter has undergone in the dream. . . In our memories we have more or less true pictures, in our dreams transformed pictures, of outer life. That is one kind of dream.

There is however another kind, and this is really much more characteristic for a knowledge of dream-life. It is the kind in which, for example, a man dreams of seeing a row of white pillars, one of which is damaged or dirty; he wakes up with this dream and finds he has toothache. He then realizes that the row of pillars 'symbolizes' the row of teeth; one tooth is aching, and this is represented by the damaged or, perhaps, dirty pillar. Or a person may wake up dreaming of a seething stove, and find he has palpitation of the heart. Or he is distressed in his dream by a frog approaching his

hand; he takes hold of the frog and finds it soft. He shudders, and
wakes up to find he is holding a corner of his blanket, grasped in
sleep. These things can go much further. He may dream of all kinds
of snake-like forms, and wake up with intestinal pains. So we see
that this second kind of dream gives pictorial, symbolic expression to man's inner organs. When we have grasped this, we learn
to interpret many dream-figures in just this way. . .

Here indeed is something that points very clearly to the whole
inner life of man. There are people who, while actually dreaming, compose subjects out of the dream for quite good paintings.
If you have studied these things you will know what particular
organ is depicted, though in an altered, symbolic form. Such paintings sometimes possess unusual beauty; and when the artist is told
what organ he has actually symbolized so beautifully, he is quite
startled, for he has not the same respect for his organs that he has
for his paintings. . .

Now it is comparatively easy to pursue the study of dreams
as far as this. Most people whose attention has been called to the
existence of these two kinds will recall experiences of their own
that justify this classification.

But to what does this classification point? Well, if you examine
the first kind of dream, studying a little the special kind of pictures, you find that widely different outer experiences can be represented by the same dream; again, one and the same experience
can be depicted in different people by different dreams. Take the
case of a man who dreams he is approaching a mountain. There
is a cave-like opening into which the sun is still shining. He dreams
he goes in. It soon begins to grow dark, then quite dark. He gropes
his way forward, meets an obstacle, and feels there is a small lake
in front of him. He is in great danger, and the dream takes a dramatic course. Now a dream like this can represent very different outer
experiences. It may relate to a railway accident in which the
dreamer was once involved; the pictures are quite different from
what he experienced. Or he could have been in a shipwreck, or
a friend may have proved unfaithful, and so on. If you compare
the dream-picture with the actual experience in this intimate way,
you will find that the content of the pictures is not really of great
importance; it is the *dramatic sequence* that is significant: whether
a feeling of expectation was present, whether this is relieved or

leads to a crisis. One might say the whole complex of feelings is translated into the dream-life.

Now if we start from here and examine dreams of this first type, we find that the pictures derive their whole character chiefly from the nature of the person himself, from the individuality of his *ego*. . . If we have an understanding of dreams (not of dream-interpretation) we can often learn to know a man better than from observing his external life. When we study all that the nature of man comprises in such dreams, it always points back to the experience of the ego in the outer world.

On the other hand, when we study the second kind of dream, we find that what it conjures before the soul is experienced only in a dream. . . In ordinary day-consciousness, man experiences very little, or nothing at all, of his internal organism. The second kind of dream fundamentally puts his whole organism before him in pictures, though in transformed pictures.

Now if we study a man's life, we find that it is more or less governed by his ego, according to his strength of will and character. But the activity of the ego in life resembles very strongly the first kind of dream experience. Try to examine closely whether a person's dreams are such that in them experiences are greatly, violently altered. In anyone who has such dreams you will find a man of strong will-nature. On the other hand, a man who dreams his life almost as it actually is, not altering it in his dreams, will be found to be a man of weak will. Thus you see the action of the ego within a man's life expressed in the way he shapes his dreams. . . Now, in sleep the ego and astral body are outside the physical and etheric bodies. The ego then takes hold in the dream of the pictures of waking life, pictures that it otherwise takes hold of in ordinary reality through the physical and etheric bodies. The first kind of dream is an activity of the ego outside the physical and etheric bodies.

What, then, is the second kind of dream? Of course it too must have something to do with what is outside the physical and etheric bodies during sleep; and it cannot be the ego, because this knows nothing of the symbolic organ-forms presented by the dream. One is forced to see that it is the *astral body* that shapes these symbolic pictures of the inner organs in the dream, as the ego shapes the pictures of outer experience. Thus the two kinds of dream point to an activity of the ego and astral body between falling asleep and waking up.

We can go further. . .

Twofold are the forces in man.
One stream of force goes inward,
This gives form and inner root of being.
One stream of force goes outward,
This gives well-being and life's radiant light.
If forces of the heavy body-man torment you,
Think yourself as buoyant man of light.

3

FROM DEATH TO REBIRTH

1. READING TO THE DECEASED

A person who dies may not during his earthly life have known anthroposophy, but his brother, his wife, or a close friend is perhaps an anthroposopher. The person who has died has refused during life to have anything to do with anthroposophy, may perhaps have abused it. He then passes through the portal of death, and can now be acquainted with anthroposophy through the other people on Earth, but in this case there must be someone on Earth who gives it to the other out of love, so that the connection with the Earth is preserved. Upon this rests what I have called 'Reading to the Dead'. We can do them a great service by this, even though previously they wished to know nothing about the spiritual world. We can do it either in the form of thought, instructing the dead, or we may take an anthroposophical book or something similar, picture those who have died, and read to them. The dead can then perceive it... One may also have the experience which came to me recently; I was asked about one who had died, because he made his presence felt by all sorts of signs, particularly during the night, by disquiet in the room, rattling, etc. From this it may often be concluded that the departed wants something. In this case it did actually turn out that the departed one *was* longing for something. During his life he had been a learned man, but had rejected all that came to him as knowledge of the spiritual world. It was now realized that a great service would be done to him if a definite course of lectures were read to him, because the things he thirsted for are discussed in it. In this extremely important way, a remedy which extends beyond death can be provided for something which has been neglected on Earth.

Such experiences bring home to us the great and important mission, that anthroposophy will bridge the gulf between the living and the dead, so that when people die it will not be as if they went away from us, but we shall still be connected with them and be able to do something for them. Should anyone enquire if we always know whether the departed hears us, we must reply that those who do this devotedly will really notice after a time, from the way in which the thoughts they read to the dead live in their own soul, that the departed one is near them. This however, is a feeling which can only be perceived by sensitive souls. The worst thing that can happen in such a case, which may be a great labour of love, is that it is not listened to; it has then been done to no purpose for the one concerned, but perhaps it had some other significance in the order of the world. One ought not to trouble too much about such a lack of success, for it often happens that something is read here to a number of people, and neither do they listen!

We must continually emphasize the fact that the way we shall live in the spiritual world after death will depend entirely on the manner in which we have lived here upon Earth. Social life with other human beings in the spiritual world will also depend on the kind of relationship we have tried to form with them here. In the other world we cannot, without more ado, make a connection with a person with whom we had no connection here. The possibility of being brought to him, of being with him in the spiritual world, is acquired as a rule through the connections made here on Earth, not however merely through those made in the last incarnation, but also in former ones. In short, actual and personal relationships which we have had on Earth determine our life between death and rebirth...

May love of hearts reach out to love of souls,
May warmth of love ray out to spirit-light.
Even so would we draw near to you,
Thinking with you thoughts of spirit,
Feeling in you love of worlds,
Consciously at one with you,
Willing in silent being.

2. CONVERSE WITH THE DEAD

The life we lead in the spiritual world between death and rebirth is very different from what we undergo here between birth and death. Pictures drawn from earthly life therefore, however well conceived, will always be inadequate to characterize man's real spiritual life. Only slowly and gradually can we be led to an understanding of what, in spiritual worlds, is reality.

Suppose for example a person leaves his earthly body and with his soul-spiritual life enters the world of soul and spirit. Suppose also that someone here on Earth has achieved initiation-knowledge in a more intimate sense, and can observe souls further in their life after death. Much preparation is necessary for this; a certain destiny connecting the person on Earth with the one yonder is also essential. Now it is a question of gaining some means of mutual understanding with the one who has died. I am speaking here of extraordinarily difficult spiritual experiences; for it is easier in general to describe the universe in its spiritual aspect than to come at all near to one who has died, although people easily believe that this is not so.

To begin with, we can only communicate with the dead by entering into their capacity of memories for the physical world. They still retain an echo of human speech, even of the particular language which was mainly theirs while on Earth, but their relation to language changes. For instance, in conversing with one who has died we notice that they very soon have no understanding for nouns, substantives. The living may address such words to them; the dead, if I may use this expression, simply do not hear them. Verbs on the other hand, words expressing action, they understand for a comparatively long time.

As a rule you will only become able to converse with the dead if you know how to put your questions. You often have to proceed as follows. One day you concentrate on the person as quietly as you can, you try to live with him in something really definite, for after death he has in his soul pictures rather than abstract notions. Therefore you must concentrate on some real experience which he was glad to have had here in earthly life; thus you gradually get near him. You will not as a rule get an immediate answer, you often have to sleep on it, perhaps several times; after some days you get the answer. But you will never get an answer if you ask in nouns. You must take pains to clothe all nouns in verbal form; such preparation is indispensible. He will most readily understand verbs, especially if you make them pictorial and vivid. The dead will never understand for instance the word 'table', but if you imagine vividly what is astir while a table is being made — a process of becoming, therefore — you will gradually become intelligible to him, so that he apprehends your question and you get an answer. The answers too will always be in verbal form, or perhaps not even that; they may only consist of what we on Earth call interjections, exclamations.

Above all, the dead speak in actual sound, sounds of the alphabet and combinations of sounds. The longer a soul has lived in the spiritual world after death, the more will he be speaking in a kind of language you can only master by cultivating a true feeling of discrimination for earthly speech, no longer insisting on the abstract meaning of words but entering into their feeling-content. With the sound 'a' (as in father) we experience something like astonishment and wonder. When we say not only 'a' but 'ach' (as in Bach) we take the sense of wonder deep into the soul; 'ach' signifies: 'a', I feel wonder; 'ch', the sense of wonder goes right into me. And if I now put 'm' before it and say 'mach' (make), I follow what awakens wonder in me as though it were coming nearer to me step by step, 'mmm', until I am entirely within it. It is with this *kind* of meaning, which issues from the sounds themselves, that the answers of the dead will often come.* The dead do not speak English, nor German nor Russian; their speech is such that only heart and soul can understand them — if heart and soul are in ears that hear.

I said before that the human heart is greater and more majestic than the Sun. From the earthly aspect it is true that the heart is somewhere inside us, and will be no pretty sight if we excise it anatomically. Yet the real heart is present throughout the human being, permeating all the organs; so it is also in the ear. We must get used to the heart-language of the dead, if I may so describe it. We do so by gradually learning to jettison all nouns and noun-like forms, and live in verbs. It is words of action and becoming which the dead still understand for a comparatively long time after

*Details may be found in *Eurythmy as Visible Speech*.

death. At a later stage they understand something which is no longer language in the ordinary sense, and what we then receive from them has first to be retranslated into an earthly language.

3. REINCARNATION AND DARWINISM

I cannot understand the soul of Newton, unless I conceive it as coming from a previous being of soul. And this soul-being can never in any event be sought in the physical ancestors; for if you were to seek it there, you would turn the whole spirit of natural science on its head. How could a scientist agree that one animal species had developed out of another, if the latter were as dissimilar from the former as Newton was in soul from his ancestors? Our supposition is that one species develops from another similar one that stands only a single stage below it. Thus Newton's soul must have come from one that was similar, but as a soul only one stage lower. Newton's soul-element is expressed for me in his biography. I recognize Newton from his biography, as I recognize a lion from the description of its species. And I understand the lion species when I imagine that it has developed out of one which is lower in comparison to it. Thus I understand what I grasp of Newton's biography when I think of it as having developed out of a biography that is similar to it and is related to it as a soul. Thus Newton's soul was already there in another form, as the lion species was already there in another form.

For clear thinking there is no escape from this view. Because current scientific opinion does not have the courage to carry its thoughts through to the end, it does not however reach this conclusion. But through this the reappearance of the being which one grasps through its biography is assured. Either one gives up the whole scientific theory of evolution, or one accepts that it must be extended to soul development. There are only two options: either each soul is created by miracle, as animal species must be created by miracle if they have not evolved from one another, or the soul has evolved, and was previously present in another form, as the animal species was there in another form . . .

Later conditions are the results of earlier ones — indeed the later physical conditions are the result of earlier physical conditions, but also the later soul conditions are the result of previous soul conditions. This is the content of the *law of karma*, which says: Everything that I can do and do in my present life is not there on its own through a miracle, but is connected as effect with the previous forms of existence of my soul, and as cause with a subsequent one. Those who regard human life with an open spiritual eye and do not know this law continually stand before riddles of life. . .

Only he who recognizes evolution in the soul-spiritual realm has a right to speak of this evolution in the realm of outer nature. It is now clear that this recognition, this extension of the knowledge of nature beyond nature, is more than mere cognition. For it transforms knowing into *life;* it not only enriches man's knowledge, but gives him the strength to tread his path in life. It shows him whence he came and whither he is going. And this whence and whither points him outwards beyond birth and death, if he follows consistently the direction which the knowledge shows him. He knows that everything he does is incorporated into a stream flowing from eternity to eternity. Ever higher and higher becomes the viewpoint from which he regulates his life. Man is as if enveloped in a dull cloud before he comes to this conviction, for he knows nothing of his true being, nothing of its origin nor of its aims. He follows the impulses of his nature, without having insight into these impulses. He must say to himself that he would perhaps follow quite other impulses, if his path were illumined with the light of knowledge. The feeling of responsibility for life grows ever greater under the influence of such a conviction. If a man does not, however, cultivate this feeling of responsibility within him, he in a higher sense denies his humanity. Knowledge without the aim of the ennoblement of mankind is the mere satisfaction of higher desires. To raise knowledge to the grasping of the spirit, so that it becomes strength for the whole of life, is in a higher sense a duty. And hence it is a duty for every man to seek for the 'whence and whither' of the soul.

4. BETWEEN DEATH AND REBIRTH

In the spiritual world between death and rebirth we are among purely spiritual beings; partly with those whose whole existence is in the spiritual world, who never incorporate in earthly substance, among whom belong those of the higher Hierarchies —

Angels, Exusiai, Seraphim and Cherubim. . .* and partly with the souls of men who have cast off their earthly bodies and taken on spiritual ones; or with those souls who are awaiting their coming redescent to earth. This depends somewhat on whether we have formed a bond with such souls in earthly life; for those persons with whom we have not been in close contact on Earth have little to do with us in the spiritual world. Then, too, a man stands in relation to other beings who never incorporate so directly in earthly life as he himself, for they are at a lower stage and do not achieve human form; these are the elemental beings who live in the kingdoms of nature. Thus between death and rebirth a man grows together with this whole spirit-populated world. . .

Now picture vividly: in the life between death and a new birth a man is active. Through his activity, every action by the soul, every grasping, one might say every touch, immediately changes into a cosmic thought, so that in doing anything we imprint it on the spiritual world. Then on all sides an answer rings back from the cosmos: out of what we do, there flashes up what the cosmos says of it, and this cosmic verdict stands there.

But that is not all. In this flashing up of the cosmic world of thought, something else glimmers, other thoughts which we cannot say originate in the cosmos. Thus we find the brilliantly flashing thoughts permeated by all sorts of dark thoughts, glimmering out of our surroundings. While the brightly gleaming thoughts from the cosmos fill us with a profound feeling of pleasure, the glimmering ones very often, thought not always, carry something extraordinarily disquieting; for they are thoughts still working on from our own life on Earth. If we have cultivated good thoughts they glimmer out from the radiant cosmic environment; if we have cherished bad thoughts, evil thoughts, they glimmer out towards us from the shining thoughts of the cosmic verdict. In this way we behold both what the cosmos is saying to us and what we ourselves have brought with us to the cosmos. This is not a world that detaches itself from a person; it remains intimately bound up with him. After death he bears within him his cosmic existence and, as a memory, his last existence on Earth.

*Rudolf Steiner adheres to the traditional Christian nomenclature derived from Dionysius the Areopagite, in the School of St Paul.

As long as we are in that region of spiritual experience which in my book *Theosophy* I called the soul-world, we are always pre-occupied with this aftermath of glimmering earthly thoughts, earthly ways of life, earthly aptitudes. Because of this we make what we feel could be beautiful cosmic forms into grotesque ones; and so during our passage through the soul-world under the guid-ance of these distorted cosmic forms, uneasily adjusting and being adjusted, we wander on through the cosmos until we are freed from everything binding us to the Earth. . .

Existence in the soul-world is essentially a living backwards through all that we have slept through in unconscious imagery during our nights on Earth. One third of the duration of a man's earthly life is thus spent in weaning himself from that which his glimmering thoughts carry into the thoughts of the cosmos. Dur-ing this time he experiences his coming into relation with the world of the stars, and especially with the Moon. . . The reason why we do not simply circle round the Moon but move on to approach another state of existence is partly the onward driving force of the Mercury beings. These beings are rather stronger than those of Venus. Existence is urged forward by the Mercury beings, where-as through the Venus beings it is dammed back, as though given fullness. Hence the essential course of a man's passage through the soul-world is such that he feels taken up into the activity of Moon, Mercury, Venus.

We must make a clear picture of this form of existence. . . After death we say: 'As a man I consist of what comes from the Moon-spirits' — this corresponds with our saying on Earth: ' I have a head'. And whereas on Earth we say: 'I have a heart in my breast', which covers the whole breathing and circulatory system, in the soul-world we say: 'I bear within me the forces of Venus'. Again whereas on Earth we say: 'I have a metabolic-limb system with all its organs', of which the chief is the kidney-system, after death we have to say: 'The forces coming from the Mercury beings live in me'. Thus on Earth we say: 'As man I am head, breast, lower body and limbs'; and after death: 'As man I am Moon, Venus, Mercury'. . .

When a man has completed the first revolution in the realm of the Moon he comes to the Sun realm, and the spiritual Sun then stands in the same relation to him as the Moon did previously. He must now, on entering what in my book *Theosophy* I called spirit-land, transform his existence and become quite a different being. . . On entering this realm we find the Sun to be no longer in a definite place, it is everywhere. A man is then within the Sun. It shines in upon him from the periphery, and is in fact the spiritual skin of the entity he has become. Moreover he has what must again be described as organs, which we must attribute to Mars, Jupiter, Saturn. These new organs, not fully formed when we first enter the world of spirit from the soul-world, have now to be gradually developed. For this we do not describe only one revolution but three, in which the Mars organ, the Jupiter organ and the Saturn organ are developed. These are traversed about 12 times more slowly than the Moon circle. Just as we are active on Earth with the forces of nature, so there we are active with the beings of the higher Hierarchies, whose physical manifestations such as sun and moon in the starry heavens are only an outer reflection. . .

It is with the Hierarchy of Angels, Archangels and Archai that a man is essentially concerned during his Moon existence after death, while the higher Hierarchies are still beyond his knowledge. The judgements of the Angels are especially important for the deeds of individual men, and it is from the Angels that a man learns the value his own deeds have in the cosmos as a whole. From the Archangels he learns more about the value of what he has done in connection with the language he speaks, with the people to whom he belongs, and from this source also come impulses which work into his further destiny. From the Archai he learns what value his actions during a given period on Earth will have for the time when he has to descend once more into earthly existence.

By means of all that a man can acquire in this way if — and I beg you to bear this in mind — he has rightly prepared himself for life after death through all the impulses he is able to receive on Earth, and particularly through his attitude towards the great leaders of mankind, he can then find his way over from the sphere of the Moon-dwellers to the sphere of the Sun-dwellers. . . In the Moon sphere he comes to know what he is destined to be in his next earthly existence, though the actual preparations cannot be made for it at that stage. For this he has to rise to the sphere of the Sun. . .

On coming into the vast sphere of the Sun, where our interests are substantially widened, we are able to work with the Exusiai, Dynamis and Kyriotetes on preparing the spirit-germ of a physical body which can then be born for us from suitable parents... Our essential work there — a work far greater and more comprehensive than anything achieved during our little life on Earth — is to concern ourselves together with beings of a higher degree, with all that takes place among these beings as spiritual events, just as here there are natural events; with all that takes place in them as art of the spirit, just as here we have the art of nature. All this finally enables us to bring together what has thus been worked at into a great, spiritual, archetypal picture which is the spirit-germ, the foreshadowing, of what will later be born on Earth as our physical body...

This spirit-germ is at first majestic and as great as the cosmos itself. While a man is making his return journey to the physical world, and watching the generations through which his parents descend, and while from the spiritual world he participates in this sequence of generations, the germ becomes smaller and smaller... When it has at last been sent down to the parents at the end of its long journey from the spiritual world, the man himself, still in the spiritual world, gathers ether substance around him there, so that for a time he becomes a being of ego, astral body and ether, the ether having been drawn together from the whole world ether. It is not until the embryonic period, during the third or fourth week after conception, that the human being unites with the organism that has been formed by combining the spirit-germ with the physical germ, and bestows upon it the etheric body drawn from the world ether. Man then becomes a being composed of physical body, an etheric body drawn together in the last stages of his cosmic existence, and the astral body and ego which have gone through the life between death and rebirth. Thus, after experiencing the purely spiritual, a man descends to another existence in the physical world.

If to the spirit of cosmic being
You strive to direct your attention,
Then will you find yourself

Free man in the realm of fate.
But if you turn away from this,
And only keep your mind attuned ·
To the daily semblance-nature,
Then you will, as image of man,
Lose yourself in the play of fate.

5. THE REVALUATION OF HISTORY

When we look back over the historical evolution of mankind, in which event follows event in the course of the ages, we are nowadays accustomed to regard these events as though we might find in more recent times the effects and results of earlier ages, as though we could speak of cause and effect in history in the same way as we do in connection with the external physical world. We are however bound to admit that when we do look at history in this way, nearly all of it remains unexplained. We shall not, for example, succeed in explaining the Great War simply as an effect of the events that took place from the beginning of the century until the year 1914. Neither shall we succeed in explaining the French Revolution at the end of the eighteenth century out of the events that preceded it. Many theories of history are put forward, but they do not carry us very far, and in the last resort we cannot but deem them artificial.

Events in human history only become capable of explanation in reality when we look at the personalities who play a decisive part in bringing about these events, in respect of their repeated lives on Earth. And only when we have taken the trouble to observe for a considerable time the karma of such historical personages as it shows itself in the course of their lives on Earth shall we acquire the right mood of soul to go into the matter of our own karma. Let us then today study karma a little as it shows itself in history. We will take a few historical persons who have done something or other known to us, and see how what we know may be traced from that which was written into their karma from their earlier incarnations.

It will in this way become clear to us that the things that happen in one epoch of history have really been brought over by human beings from earlier epochs. And as we learn to take quite seriously — it is too often considered as mere theory — all that is said about karma and repeated Earth-lives, as we come to place it before us in precise and concrete detail, we shall be able to say: All of us have been on the Earth many times before, and we have brought with us into this present Earth-life the fruits of earlier Earth-lives. It is only when we have learned to be quite earnest about this that we have any right to speak of the perception of karma as something that we *know*. But the only way to learn to perceive karma is to take the ideas of karma and put them as great questions to the history of man. Then we shall no longer say: What happened in 1914 is the result of what happened in 1910, and what happened in 1910 is the result of what happened in 1900, and so on. Then we shall try instead to understand how the personalities who make their appearance in life themselves bring over from earlier epochs that which shows itself in a later one. It is only on this path that we shall arrive at a true and genuine study of history, beholding the external events we meet against the background of human destinies.

History sets us such a number of riddles! But many a riddle is cleared up if we set about studying it in the way described. People appear sometimes quite suddenly in history like meteors, we are astonished that they appear at a certain time. We examine their education and upbringing — it affords no explanation as to why they appear in this way. We examine the age to which they belong — again we can find no clue to the problem of their appearance in this particular way. Karmic connections alone afford an explanation.

DESTINY AND INNER REALITY

1. PRACTICAL WORKING OF KARMA

When you look back to your childhood, you will certainly have
to admit that you have brought about many changes in your
character since then. But at the same time you will realize that
observation of your characteristics, and learning how to change
them, are processes related to each other, as are the minute hand
of the clock and the hour hand. . . Whatever lights up in us tem-
porarily and disappears again has its seat in the astral body. But
what becomes a man's permanent stock in life, in so far as it comes
to expression in the soul, everything that becomes a habit so that
it is noticeable in a person for a long time — perhaps always —
in his life, everything that has to do with the temperament, is situated in the etheric body, which is denser than the astral body. . .
When someone accepts a moral principle but is obliged to say to
himself repeatedly 'the principle exists, so that is why I obey it'
then it is still only rooted in the astral body. But if it draws into
him to such an extent that he can simply do no other, then it is
established in the etheric body. The transition from the astral body
to the etheric body takes place slowly and gradually in life.

What takes place during the same life on Earth only slowly,
namely the transition of something at first only in the astral body
into the etheric body, happens karmically from one incarnation
to another in the following way. Whoever has tried to judge things
correctly in accordance with morality, and who in doing so may
perhaps still have been prompted by other considerations, finds
the fruits of this striving in his next life as a basic quality of his
etheric body, as a kind of habit, as a quality of character. . .
Propensities and *habits* stem from ideas, thoughts and concepts

formed in previous lives. If you pay attention to this, you can make provision for the next incarnation by laying the foundation of a definite organization of the etheric body. You can say to yourself: I shall try in this life to say to myself over and over again that this or that is right and good. Then the etheric body will ultimately show you that it is good and right in the very nature of things to follow the principle concerned.

*A concept that can be explained in the light of karma is important here. It is the concept of *conscience*. What arises from a man's conscience is equally something that has been acquired. He has a conscience, an instinct for what is good, right and true, only because in his past lives, in his experiences during life, in his moral principles, he has built up this conscience. You can provide for the strengthening and enhancement of conscience if you undertake to deepen every day your moral conceptions. Moral conceptions become conscience in the next and subsequent life. So you see that what the minute hand of life shows us becomes the hour hand in the next life. There need only be a certain repetition of the moral principles and ideas in one life, and then they are consolidated for the next.

What is established in the etheric body of one life brings to maturity fruits for the *physical body* of the next life. Good habits, good inclinations, good traits of character prepare healthiness, physical proficiency, physical strength, therefore a healthy physical body, for the next life. A healthy physical body in one life indicates that the person concerned prepared this in an earlier life through self-acquired habits and qualities of character. A particularly strong connection exists between a well-developed memory in one life and the physical body in the next... Whoever develops his memory conscientiously will be reborn with physical soundness, with limbs that can be truly useful to him for giving effect to what his soul inwardly desires. A body that cannot achieve this stems from a previous life during which no care was given to developing a good and healthy memory, but when through slovenliness it was left to be forgetful.

Today we are speaking only of single phenomena, but you can realize the magnitude of the whole domain of which we are speaking... What I have put before you are not theories, but definite cases that have been tested; they are based on specific results of research... Facts alone are being presented...

An individual whose past life was fraught with tainted qualities of character has thus in this life an organism that is more easily prone to physical *illnesses*. One who was equipped with healthy characteristics and a sound temperament will be reborn with a body that can be exposed to every possible epidemic without being infected. You see therefore that things in the world are in a complex way subject to the law of cause and effect. For example, here is a case based on definite results of investigation. A person had developed an entirely egoistic urge for acquisition, a veritable greed for external wealth. It was not a matter of a healthy striving for riches, which may spring from an altruistic aim to be of help and engage in selfless activity in the world — that is something different — but an egoistic longing for acquisition which was abnormal, due to a particular constitution of the etheric body. Such a person will often be born in the next life with a physical body prone to catch infectious diseases. In numerous cases it has been established by spiritual research that people readily prone to infection from epidemics in the present life had a pathological sense for acquisition in the previous life.

Other examples could be quoted. Thus there are two characteristics which have a clearly recognizable influence on the karmic formation of the following life. We must speak first of the strong influence exerted by a loving, benevolent attitude towards one's fellow men. In many cases this extends far beyond pure human kindness to a love of nature and of the whole world. The more strongly this all-embracing love has developed and become habit in the soul, hence rooted in the etheric body, the greater becomes the capacity to retain the qualities of youth for a long time in a subsequent incarnation... A body that shows the signs of age at a physically early age stems from the life of a perverse critic, from a life of aversion and ill-will. Thus we see that life can be influenced by a conscious intervention in karma...

One who achieves occult development learns how to influence not only his astral body but also his etheric body and his physical body. Through the transformation of habitual behaviour, an irascible individual can become gentle, a highly emotional person an equable, harmonious human being. An esotericist must change his habits in a comparatively short time. Genuine development presupposes that what a man learns does not remain mere teaching but penetrates into the etheric body. A process that in ordinary life is distributed over many incarnations is shortened: the process of karma itself is shortened...

Suffering in the preceding life — physical and also soul suffering — becomes *beauty* in a subsequent life, beauty of the external physical body. Here it is permissible to use an analogy: how does the beautiful pearl originate in an oyster? Actually as the result of an illness. Approximately speaking, there is a karmic process which represents the connection of illness, of suffering, with beauty. This beauty is often bought at the cost of suffering and illness. Wisdom too is in many respects bought at the cost of pain. It is not without interest that outer investigation today confirms what occultists have said for thousands of years, namely that wisdom is connected with pain and sufferings, with a life of earnestness and renunciation in the previous existence...

We must strictly differentiate between all a man accomplishes as his own deeds, deeds which proceed entirely from himself, and those made obligatory by his race, family and profession. Two councillors may do the same thing because they are councillors, but that is not the point. They may however also perform utterly different deeds because they are different people, and that is what concerns us now. Deeds that stem from a man's personality, that is what meets him as his outer *destiny* in the next incarnation. If someone finds himself in fortunate circumstances in life, if he enjoys a favourable destiny, this leads back to the just, ingenious, and good deeds of an earlier life. If a man's circumstances in life are unfavourable, if he has many failures and is surrounded by adverse conditions — external circumstances are meant, not qualities of the physical body — this equally leads back to personal deeds of the previous life. What a person has accomplished as the result of his vocation and family circumstances lies in his temperament and character. Thus the destiny of a man is determined by his personal deeds. Through good, intelligent and righteous deeds he can bring about a favourable destiny in the next incarnation.

An individual who comes into contact with particular personalities has himself created the conditions for this in a preceding life. He had something to do with them, and has himself now led them into his environment. Here is an example from the time of the Vehmic tribunals.* One such tribunal concerned an execution. The victim was placed before masked judges, who immediately gave judgement. This is a case where a man was condemned and executed. Investigation of his destiny in earlier incarnations showed that the individual executed by the five judges had once as a chieftain allowed these five persons to be killed. His deed had again brought these five men as if with magnetic force into his life, and they wreaked their vengeance upon him. This is a radical case, but it is founded on a universal law. You cannot come into contact with a person who makes an impact on your life, if you have not yourself brought him into your orbit on the basis of earlier relationships. It may of course also be the case that through general conditions, through vocation or family, a man is led into contact with individuals he has never yet encountered; but then, through their mutual conduct, the foundation is laid for a meeting in the next incarnation, a meeting connected with the destinies and lives of the individuals concerned. You will realize that these illustrations of karma are in many respects complicated and by no means easy to explain. It is important to study these examples individually, because only so can we really understand life.

It must be repeatedly stressed that the idea of karma, rightly understood, must never be thought to contradict the teaching of the Redemption to be found in Christianity. . . Karma is a kind of life account that may well be compared with a merchant's accounts. On the one side there are the debit entries and on the other the credit entries. They are added and a balance struck. . . Just as in every moment of a merchant's life a new transaction can be made, so at every moment through a new deed new karma can be created. If someone says that a man has himself brought about his suffering, he deserved it so I may not help him, this is nonsense. It is as if one were to say to a bankrupt merchant: five thousand pounds would help you, but if I were to give them to you I should upset your account book! The sum would simply be entered in the account. It is the same with life. Karma does not signify self-compensation, but only compensation through a deed. Now suppose you are a wealthy, powerful person who can help not only one but two. Then you can intervene in the karma of the two; just because karma exists you can intervene in the life accounts

*A system in Westphalia in the fourteenth and fifteenth centuries.

of both. There are individuals who can help three, four, five people, indeed even hundreds.

Such help can be vouchsafed by a most mighty being who once appeared in the world, to those who account themselves His followers. This is Christ Jesus. The fact that the Redemption was brought about by certain forms of evil does not contravene the law of karma. The Redemption through Christ Jesus is fully compatible with the law of karma, just as is the help given by a wealthy man to the bankrupt merchant. It is precisely through the intrinsic nature and importance of the deed of a single sublime being that the continuation of the law of karma is guaranteed.* When in the future these things are rightly understood, will it first become evident that anthroposophy is not an opponent of any confession that has a genuine foundation, and that far rather it leads to a true understanding of it.

If you have discerned the law of karma in a certain number of cases, you will feel that you have here perceived a deep necessity of spiritual life. The law of karma is rightly understood only by one for whom it is not merely theoretic knowledge, but who has made it part of his whole world of feeling and perception. Inner security and harmony then pervade the whole of life... To live in accordance with the law of karma means to infuse courage and hope into the soul.

The law of karma must above all throw light upon our future. We must think less about the past than about the future. It has been indicated in many ways that a man can produce effects far into the future in compliance with the law of karma, by preparing in his astral body the future configuration of the etheric body, and in the course of further progress the future foundation of the physical body. When you have grasped the implications of this you will realize the tremendous importance of these connections...

* See also Chapter 6. 3 — 'The Lord of Karma'.

Joys are gifts of destiny
Which reveal their worth in the present
But sufferings are sources of knowledge
Whose meaning shows itself in the future.

2. THE STRANGER WHO GOES WITH US

When we have our inner life in mind, we can distinguish two
groups of experiences: in one we are aware of the causes of our
successes and failures; in the second we cannot detect any such
connection, and it will seem more or less chance that we failed
in one instance and succeeded in another. Or if we have more in
mind our destiny in outer life, we find cases where it is inwardly
clear to us that in connection with events which befell us — not
those we initiated — we did certain things and are responsible for
what happened; but in others we can see no connection whatever
with what we intended, and it is usually said that they broke in
upon our life as if by chance. . .

. A kind of experiment can be made with these two groups of
experiences. We ask ourselves: How would it be if we were to build
up in thought a kind of imaginary person, ascribing to him just
those things for which we can see no connection with our own
faculties: we endow this imaginary man with the qualities and
faculties which have led to these happenings incomprehensible to
us. We imagine a man possessing faculties such that he will inevitably succeed or fail in matters where we cannot say this of ourselves, one who has quite deliberately brought about the events
which seem to have come into our life by chance. Simple examples can serve as a starting-point. Suppose a tile from a roof has
fallen upon and injured our shoulder. We should be inclined to
attribute this to chance. But as an experiment, we imagine a man
who acts in the following strange way: he climbs on the roof,
loosens a tile to the point where it has only a slight hold, then runs
down quickly so that when the tile is quite loose it falls on his
shoulder! The same can be done for all events which seem to have
come into our life by chance. We build up an imaginary man who
is guilty of or brings about all those events of which in ordinary
life we cannot see their connection with us.

To do this may at first seem nothing but a play of fancy. No obligation is incurred by doing it. But such a man makes a quite remarkable impression upon us. We cannot get rid of the picture we have thus created; although it seems so artificial, it fascinates us, and gives the impression that it must have something to do with us. The feeling we have for this imaginary man ensures this. If we steep ourselves in this picture, it will most certainly not leave us free. A remarkable process then takes place within our feeling mind. We may compare this with something which often happens: suppose we need to recall something, and use all sorts of artificial means for doing so. Just try to realize how many times auxiliary thoughts have to be used and dropped again in order to get at what we want to remember: the purpose of these auxiliary thoughts is to open the way to the recollection we need. In exactly the same but in a far more comprehensive sense, the imaginary thought-man described represents an 'auxiliary process'. He never leaves us; he is at work in such a way that we realize that he lives in us as a thought, as something that goes on working, that is actually transformed within us into the idea, the thought which now flashes up suddenly, as in the ordinary process of recollection; it floods over us.

It is as though something says to us, 'this being cannot remain as he is, he transforms himself within you, he becomes alive, he changes!' This force itself upon us in such a way (try it!) that he whispers to us, 'This is something that has to do with an Earth-existence other than the present one'. A kind of awareness of another Earth-existence — *that* thought quite definitely arises. It is more a feeling than a thought, a sentient experience, but it is as if we feel what arises in the feeling mind to be what we ourselves once were in an earlier incarnation on this Earth . . .

Again, our experiences of life can be divided into groups in different ways. One group may include the sufferings, sorrows and obstacles we have encountered, while a second includes the joys, happinesses and advantages in our life. Being what we are in this incarnation, our sorrows and sufferings are misfortunes which we would gladly avoid. But by way of experiment let us not take this attitude, but assume that for a certain reason we ourselves brought about these sorrows, sufferings and obstacles, realizing that owing to our earlier lives — if there have actually been such lives — we have become in some sense more imperfect because of what we have done. After all, we do not only become more perfect through successive incarnations; when we have affronted or harmed someone, are we not more imperfect than before? We have not only affronted him, we have taken something away from ourself; as a whole personality our worth would be greater if we had not done it. Many such actions are marked on our score, and our imperfections remain because of them. If we desire to regain our worth, what must happen? We must make compensation for the affront, we must place into the world a counter-balancing deed, we must discover some means of compelling ourselves to overcome something. And if we think in this way, we can often say: These sufferings and sorrows, if we surmount them, are suited to give us strength to overcome our imperfections. Through suffering we can make progress.

In normal life we do not think in this way; we set our face against suffering. But we can also say that every sorrow, every suffering, every obstacle in life should be an indication of the fact that we have within us a man who is cleverer than we are. With our ordinary consciousness we resist sorrows and suffering, but the cleverer man leads us towards these sufferings in defiance of our consciousness, because by overcoming them we can strip off something. This may, to begin with, be an oppressive thought, but it carries with it no obligations; we can if we wish use it once only, as a trial. In this way we are led to the result which many find disturbing, namely that this cleverer man guides us always towards what we do not like. This, then, we will take as an assumption: there is a cleverer man within us who guides us to what we do not like, in order that we may make progress.

But let us still do something else. Let us take our joys, our advantages, our happinesses, and say to ourselves, again as an experiment: 'How would it be if you were to conceive the idea — irrespective of how it tallies with reality — that you simply have not deserved these happinesses, these advantages; that they have come to you through the grace of higher spiritual powers'. . . Again this thought may be a bitter pill for the vain to swallow; but if a man is capable of forming such a thought in his feeling mind with all intensity, it leads to the basic feeling (because again it changes, and in so far as it is incorrect it rectifies itself): In you there lives something that lies deeper than anything you have experienced consciously, a cleverer man within you, who gladly turns to the eternal, divine spiritual powers pervading the world. Then it becomes an inner certainty that behind the outer there is an inner, higher individuality. Through such thought-exercises we become conscious of the eternal, spiritual core of our being. This is of extraordinary importance. There again we have something which it lies in our power to carry out.

In every respect anthroposophy can be a guide, not only towards knowledge of the existence of another world, but towards feeling oneself as a citizen of another world, as an individuality who passes through successive incarnations . . .

Wishes of the soul bud forth,
Deeds of the will are thriving,
Fruits of life are maturing.

I feel my fate: my fate finds me,
I feel my star: my star finds me,
I feel my aims: my aims find me.

My soul and the world are but one.

Life grows more radiant about me,
Life grows more arduous for me,
Life grows richer in me.

3. THE GUARDIAN OF THE THRESHOLD

The important experiences marking the student's ascent into higher worlds include his meeting with the Guardian of the Threshold. Strictly speaking there are not only one but two, a 'lesser' and a 'greater'. One meets the former when the connecting threads between willing, thinking and feeling begin to loosen within the finer bodies (the astral and etheric). One faces the greater Guardian of the Threshold when the sundering of connections extends to the physical parts of the body, at first to the brain. The lesser Guardian is an independent being. He is not present for a person until he has reached the corresponding stage of development. Only some of his most important characteristics can here be indicated.

The attempt will now be made to describe in narrative form

the meeting of the esoteric student with the Guardian of the Threshold. Through this meeting the student will first become aware that thinking, feeling and willing have in him become released from their inherent connection. A truly terrible spectral being stands before the student. He needs all the presence of mind and confidence in the security of his path of knowledge which he was able to acquire sufficiently in the course of his esoteric training up to now. The Guardian proclaims his significance in somewhat the following words:

'Hitherto, powers that were invisible to you ruled over you. They saw to it that in the course of your life until now each of your good actions brought its reward, and each of your evil actions had its bad results. Through their influence your character was formed from your life's experiences and your thoughts. They brought about your destiny. They determined the measure of joy and pain allotted to you in one of your incarnations according to your conduct in earlier lives. They ruled over you as the all-embracing law of karma. These powers will now release you from a part of your constraint. And you must now yourself undertake something of the work which they have hitherto carried out upon you. Many a hard blow of destiny struck you in the past. You did not know why. Each was the result of a harmful action in the course of one of your previous lives. You found joy and gladness, and took them as they came. They too were the fruits of earlier deeds. You have in your character many beautiful sides, many ugly flaws. You have brought about both, through previous experiences and thoughts. These were until now unknown to you, their effects alone being manifest to you. They, however, the karmic powers, beheld all your deeds in former lives, and all your most hidden thoughts and feelings. And they determined accordingly how you were to be, and how you now live.

'But now all the good and all the bad sides of your past lives shall be revealed to you. They were till now interwoven with your own being; they were in you, and you could not see them, just as you cannot physically see your own brain. But now they become separated from you; they detach themselves from your personality. They assume an independent form which you can see, just as you see the stones and plants of the outer world. And I am myself the being who fashioned a body out of your noble and your evil actions. My spectral form is woven out of your own life's account book.* Till now you have borne me invisibly within you. But it was well for you that this was so. For the wisdom of your hidden destiny has therefore also worked within you until now at the effacing of the hideous flaws in my form. Now that I have come forth from within you, that concealed wisdom too has left you. It will take no further care of you. It will leave the work in your hands alone. I must become a perfect and glorious being, if I am not to fall prey to corruption. And should this occur, I would drag you also down with me into a dark and corrupt world. Now your own wisdom must, if you would avoid this, become so great that it can undertake the task of that concealed wisdom which has departed from you. Once you have crossed my Threshold, I will never for an instant leave your side as a form visible to you. And whenever in future you act or think wrongly, you will at once perceive your guilt as a hideous, demonic distortion of my form. Only when you have made good all your past wrongs, and so purified yourself that further evil is quite impossible for you, only then will my being have become transformed into radiant beauty. Then too I shall again be able to unite with you as a single being, for the benefit of your future activity. My Threshold is however framed by every feeling of fear that remains within you, and by every shrinking from the strength yourself to take over full responsibility for all your thoughts and actions. So long as there is in you a trace of fear of yourself becoming the guide of your destiny, for just so long does this Threshold lack what must be built into it. And so long as a single stone is still missing, for just so long must you remain standing at this Threshold as though transfixed; or else stumble. Seek not to cross this Threshold, until you feel yourself entirely free from fear, and ready for the highest responsibility.

'Hitherto I only emerged from your own personality when death recalled you from an earthly life. But even then, my form was veiled from you. Only the powers of destiny who ruled over you beheld me, and in the intervals between death and a new birth could build in you according to my appearance the strength and

*In his *Occult Science*, Steiner says that the double may rightly be called the Guardian of the Threshold.

capacity with which you could work in a new earthly life at the beautification of my form, for your benefit and progress. It was I, too, whose imperfection ever and again constrained the powers of destiny to lead you back to a new incarnation upon Earth. I was present at your death, and it was on my account that the lords of karma ordained your rebirth. Only if through ever recurring earthly lives you had in this way unconsciously transformed me to complete perfection would you not have fallen to the powers of death, but have wholly united with me and passed over into immortality in unity with me.

'This kingdom you now enter will make you acquainted with beings of a supersensible nature. Happiness will there be your lot. But I myself must be your first acquaintance with this world, and I am your own creation. Previously I lived upon your own life, but now I am awakened through you to a separate existence, so that I stand before you as the visible standard of your future deeds. Perhaps too as your constant reproach. You could form me, but by doing so you have undertaken to transform me.'

What is here indicated, clothed in narrative, must not be understood as an allegory, but as an experience of the highest possible reality for the esoteric student.* The Guardian must warn him not to go a step further unless he feels within himself the strength to fulfil the demands contained in the above speech. However frightening the form assumed by the Guardian, it is only the effect of the student's own past life, his own character awoken out of him into independent existence. This awakening happens through the separation of will, thought and feeling. To feel for the first time that one has oneself called into existence a spiritual being is in itself an experience of the deepest significance. The preparation of the esoteric student must aim at enabling him to endure the terrible

*Author's footnote: It will be gathered that the 'Guardian of the Threshold' is an astral figure which manifests to the awakened, higher sight of the esoteric student, and spiritual science leads to this meeting. It is a practice of inferior magic to make the Guardian also visible to the physical senses. Such physical phenomena are no longer necessary for one sufficiently prepared for higher sight. And besides, anyone who without adequate preparation were to see his unredeemed karma appear as a living physical creature before his eyes would run the risk of erring into evil byways. Bulwer Lytton's *Zanoni* contains in the form of a novel a description of the Guardian of the Threshold.

sight without a trace of timidity, and at the moment of meeting to feel his full strength so increased that he can take upon himself the burden of himself beautifying the Guardian in full knowledge.

If successful, this meeting with the Guardian results in the student's next physical death being an entirely different event from death as he knew it formerly. He experiences death consciously, laying aside the physical body as a garment that is worn out, or perhaps rendered useless through a sudden rent. Thus his physical death is of special importance only for those living with him whose perception is still restricted to the world of the senses. For them the student 'dies', but for himself nothing of importance changes in his whole environment. The entire supersensible world which he has entered stood open to him before his death, and this same world confronts him after death.

4. FROM THE FIRST MYSTERY DRAMA THE PORTAL OF INITIATION — SCENE 2

A place in the open; rocks and springs. The whole surroundings are to be thought of as within the soul of Johannes Thomasius; what follows is the content of his meditation.

There sounds from springs and rocks:
        'O Man, know thou thyself!'

JOHANNES:
Thus have I heard for many years
these words of weighty meaning.
They sound to me from air and water
and ring out from foundations of the Earth.
And as in the tiny acorn secretly
lies hid the structure of the mighty oak,
so is contained at last in *these* words' power
all that my thought can comprehend
about the nature of the elements,
of souls and spirits, time and eternity.
The world and my own being
are living in the words
'O Man know thou thyself'.

(From springs and rocks there sounds:
　　　　　'O Man, know thou thyself!')

And now what is in me
grows frighteningly alive.
Around me weaves the dark,
within me yawns the night,
from the world's darkness sounds,
from the soul's blackness rings
'O Man, know thou thyself!'

(There sounds from springs and rocks:
　　　　　　'O Man, know thou thyself!')

It robs me now of self.
I alter with the hours of day,
and change myself to night.
The Earth I follow on its cosmic course.
I rumble in the thunder —
I flash within the lightning —
I am — yet, oh! I feel
already from my being separate.
I see my body's shell,
it is a foreign being there outside,
it is remote from me.
Another body hovers near;
and with its mouth I have to speak:
'He brought me bitter misery.
I gave him all my confidence.
He left me in my grief alone,
he robbed me of the warmth of life
and thrust me deep into cold earth.'
She whom I left, poor soul,
I was now she herself.
I had to suffer her ordeal.
Knowledge has lent me power
to be myself within another self.
O cruel word!
Your light put out by your own force —
'O man, know thou thyself!'

(There sounds from springs and rocks:
                    'O Man, know thou theyself!')

You lead me back again
into the circle of my being.
But how do I now see myself?
The human form is lost to me,
I see myself as raging dragon
created out of lust and greed.
And clearly I can sense
how an illusion's cloudy shape
has hid from me till now
my own appalling form.
The fierceness of my being must devour me.
And running like consuming fire
through all my veins I feel those words
which hitherto with primal power
revealed the truth of earths and suns.
They live within my pulse,
they beat within my heart,
and even in my thoughts I feel
the alien worlds ablaze as instincts wild.
This is the harvest of the words
'O Man, know thou thyself'

(There sounds from springs and rocks:
                    'O Man, know thou thyself!')

There from the dark abyss
what creature glares at me?
I feel the fetters now
which hold me chained to you.
Prometheus was not bound
to Caucasus' rock so fast
as I am chained to you.
Who are you, gruesome creature?

(There sounds from springs and rocks:
                    'O Man, know thou thyself!')

O, I can know you now.
It is myself.
Knowledge welds me to you, *deadly monster*,
(Maria enters, at first unobserved by Johannes)
Myself, the *deadly monster!*
I sought to flee from you,
and worlds have blinded me
to which I fled in folly
to free me from myself.
Blinded am I, in the blind soul, anew.
'O Man, know thou thyself!'

(There sounds from springs and rocks:
              'O Man, know thou thyself!')

(JOHANNES, as if coming to himself, sees Maria . . .)

5

EXPERIENCES OF CHRIST

1. A FIRST EXPERIENCE OF RESURRECTION

Before we descend to Earth we live a life of soul and spirit. But of that life in full reality of soul and spirit in pre-earthly existence, we have here on earth only our thoughts, concepts and mental images. These are in our soul, but in what way?. . . When with the vision of initiation we look back into our own soul, we behold the thoughts which we now have between birth and death, the thoughts of modern science, modern wisdom, and we recognize — these thoughts are the corpse of what we were before we descended to the Earth. As the dead body is to the human being in the fulness of life, so are our thoughts to what we were in soul and spirit before we came down to Earth. This is what the initiate can experience, it is a fact; it is not uttered out of any sentimental feeling, but comes before the soul which is active in knowledge with great intensity; it is not what the sentimental mystical dreamer says, who seeks experience out of some dark mystic depth of his being.

He who passes through the portals of initiation discovers these thoughts in his soul, which just because they are not alive make freedom possible; they form the whole basis of human freedom, because they have no power to compel, they are dead. Man can become a free being in our time because he has to deal not with living thoughts but with dead ones. But it is with all the tragedy of worlds that we experience these thoughts as the corpse of the soul. Before the soul came down to Earth all this which is today a corpse was alive and filled with movement. In supersensible spiritual worlds moved human souls who had either passed through death and now lived in the spiritual world, or who had not yet descended to Earth, also the beings of the divine Hierarchies above humanity, and the elemental beings underlying nature. There everything in the soul was alive, whilst here the soul has its heritage from spiritual worlds, and thought is dead.

Yet if as modern pupils of initiation we permeate ourselves with Christ, who made manifest His life in the Mystery of Golgotha, if we understand in its deepest, inmost sense the words of St Paul: 'Not I, but Christ in me', then Christ leads us even through this death. Then we penetrate into nature with our thoughts, and as we do so Christ goes with us in the spirit. He sinks our thoughts into the grave of nature — for inasmuch as our thoughts are dead, nature does indeed become a grave. Yet if with these dead thoughts we approach the minerals, the animals, the world of stars, the clouds, mountains and streams, accompanied by Christ Himself according to the word 'Not I, but Christ in me', then we experience in modern initiation, when we dive down into the quartz crystal, that the dead thought now rises again as living thought out of the crystal quartz, out of all nature. As though from the mineral tomb, thought is resurrected as living thought. The mineral world enables the spirit to resurrect in us. And as Christ leads us through the plant world everywhere, where otherwise only our dead thoughts would dwell, the living thoughts arise.*

Truly we should feel that we are sick when we go out into nature, or gaze into the starry universe with the mere calculating vision of the astronomer, and would sink our dead thoughts into the world; and it would be a sickness unto death. But if we let Christ be our companion, if accompanied by Him we carry our dead thoughts into the world of stars, sun, moon, clouds, mountains and rivers, minerals, plants, animals and the whole physical world of man, then in our vision of nature everything becomes alive, and there arises from all creation, as from a tomb, the living, healing spirit who awakens us from death, the Holy Spirit. We feel ourselves accompanied by Christ, with all that we hitherto experienced as death now revivified. We feel the living, healing Spirit speaking to us out of all the creatures of the world.

*See also Chapters 8.1 — *The Act of Knowing*, and 9.3 — *Organic Thinking as Supersensible Perception*.

These things must be regained in spiritual cognition in the new science of initiation. Then shall we grasp the Mystery of Golgotha as the meaning of all Earth existence; we shall know how in this age, when human freedom must be evolved through dead thoughts, we must be led by Christ to the knowing of nature. We shall know how Christ not only placed His own destiny upon Earth, in His death which formed part of the Mystery of Golgotha, but gave to the Earth the mighty liberation of Pentecost, in that He promised to mankind on Earth the living spirit, which through His help can arise from all things on the Earth. Our cognition remains dead — indeed it is itself sin — until we are so awakened by Christ that from all nature, from all existence in the cosmos, the living Spirit speaks to us again.

It is no formula devised by human cleverness, the Trinity of God the Father, God the Son, and God the Holy Spirit. It is a reality deeply bound up with the whole evolution of the cosmos; and it becomes for us a living, not a dead, knowledge when we bring to life within ourselves the Christ Who, as the Risen One, is the bringer of the Holy Spirit.

Then we understand how it is like an illness if we cannot see the divine out of which we are born; man must be implicitly ill to be an atheist, for he is only healthy if his whole physical nature is so focused that he can feel within him *Ex Deo Nascimur* (from God we are born) as the synthesis of his own being. And it is a stroke of destiny if in this earthly life a man does not find Christ, Who can lead him through the death that stands at the end of life's way, and through the death towards knowledge. But if we feel the *In Christo Morimur* (in Christ we die) then we also feel what is seeking to approach us through Christ's guidance. We feel how the living Spirit resurrects again out of all things, resurrects even within this earthly life. We feel ourselves alive again within this life on Earth, and we look through the portal of death through which Christ leads us, look into the life beyond death, and know now why Christ sent us the Holy Spirit. Because we can unite ourselves with the Holy Spirit while still on Earth if we let ourselves be led by Christ, we may say with certainty 'We die in Christ' when we pass through the gate of death.

Our experience here on Earth, with our knowledge of the world of nature, is indeed prophetic of the future. What would otherwise be a dead science will be resurrected by the living Spirit. Thus we may also say, when the death in knowledge is replaced by that real death which takes away our body: Having understood 'From God the Father we are Born' and 'In Christ we Die', we may say as we look forward through the gate of death, 'By the Holy Spirit we are Awakened': *Per Spiritum Sanctum Reviviscimus.*

So long as you feel pain
Which I am spared
Is Christ unrecognized
Working in the world.
For weak is still the spirit
Whilst each can only suffer
Through his own body.

2. EXCEPT YE BECOME...

The passing of the individual through successive incarnations is of importance for the collective evolution of mankind. This has advanced through successive lives in the past, and is still advancing; and parallel with it the Earth too moves forward in its evolution. The time will come when the Earth will have reached the end of its course. Then the earthly planet must fall away as physical entity from the totality of human souls, just as the human body falls away from the spirit at death, when the soul in order to continue living enters the spiritual realm which is suited to it between death and rebirth. When this is realized, it must appear as man's highest ideal to have progressed far enough at the death of the Earth to be able to reap all possible benefits which may be obtained from life on Earth.

Now forces come out of the Earth organism due to which man cannot stand up to the forces that work upon him during infancy. When this Earth has fallen away from him, a man must have progressed far enough, if he has attained his aim, to be able actually to give himself over with his whole being to the powers at present only active in him during infancy. Thus the object of evolution through successive earthly lives is gradually to make the whole individual, including the conscious part, into an expression of the powers ruling in him without his knowledge under the influence of the spiritual world during the first years of life.

The thought which takes possession of the soul after such reflections must fill it with humility, but also with a due consciousness of the dignity of man. The thought is this: man is not alone; something lives within him which constantly affords him proof that he can rise above himself to that which is already growing beyond him, and will go on doing so from one life to another. This thought can assume a more and more definite form; then it affords something supremely soothing and elevating, at the same time filling the soul with corresponding humility and modesty. What is it that man has within him in this way? Surely a higher, divine human being by whom he is able to feel himself interpenetrated, saying to himself 'He is my guide within me'.

From such a point of view it is not long before we reach the thought that by all means in our power we should strive to be in harmony with that within our being which is wiser than conscious intelligence. And we shall be referred from the directly conscious self to an extended self, in the presence of which all false pride and presumption will be subdued and extinguished. This feeling develops into another, which opens the way to accurate understanding of the way in which man is at present imperfect; and this feeling leads to the knowledge that man may become perfect, if once the more embracing spirituality ruling within him is allowed to bear the same relation to his consciousness as it bore in early childhood to the unconscious life of the soul.

Though it often happens that memory does not go back as far as the fourth year of a child's life, it may nevertheless be said that the influence of the higher spirit-sphere in the above sense lasts through the first three years. At the end of that time a child becomes capable of linking its impressions of the outer world to the ideas of its ego... It may be granted that those higher powers which direct a human being in the early years of childhood can be operative for three years; thus man is so organized during the present epoch that *only* for three years can he receive these forces...

Suppose now that a human organism were to come into the world, and later in life be freed of his ego by the action of certain cosmic powers, receiving in exchange the ego which usually works in man only during the first three years of childhood, and which would be in connection with the spiritual worlds in which man exists between death and rebirth: how long would such a person be able to live in an earthly body? About three years. For at the end of that time, something would arise through cosmic karma which would destroy the human organism in question.

What is here supposed is, however, an historical fact. The human organism which stood in the river Jordan at the baptism by John, when the ego of Jesus of Nazareth left the three bodies, contained after the baptism, in complete conscious development, that Higher Self of Humanity which usually works with cosmic wisdom on a child without its knowledge. At the same time the necessity arose, that this Self which was in connection with the higher spirit-world could only live for three years in the human organism concerned. Events had then to take place which after three years brought the earthly life of that being to a close. The outer events in the life of Christ Jesus are to be interpreted as absolutely conditioned by the inner causes just set forth, and present themselves as the outward expression of those causes. This is the deeper connection existing between that which is man's guide in life, streaming in upon our infancy like the dawn and always working below the surface of our consciousness as the best part of us, and that which once entered the whole of human evolution so that it could be for three years in a human frame.

What then is manifested in that 'higher' ego, which is in connection with the spiritual hierarchies, and which at that time entered the body of Jesus of Nazareth? This entrance was symbolically represented by the sign of the spirit descending in the form of a dove, and by the words 'this is my well-beloved Son, today have I begotten him' (for so the words stood originally). If we fix our eyes upon this picture, we are contemplating the highest human ideal. For it means nothing else than that the history of Jesus of Nazareth is a statement of this fact: Christ can be discerned in every human being...

The recognition of the forces working in human nature during infancy is the recognition of Christ in man. The question now arises, does this recognition lead to the further perception of the fact that this Christ once really dwelt on Earth in a human body? Without bringing forward any documents this question may be answered in the affirmative. For genuine clairvoyant knowledge of self leads the man of the present day to recognize that powers are to be discovered in the human soul which emanate from Christ. These powers are at work during the first three years of childhood without any action being taken by man. In later life they *can* be called into action, if Christ be sought within the soul by inner meditation. Man was not always able, as he now is, to find Christ within himself. There were times when no inner meditation could lead him to Christ. This again we learn from clairvoyant perception. In the interval between that past time when man could not find Christ in himself, and the present time when he can find him, there took place Christ's earthly life. And that life itself is the cause of man's being able to find Christ in himself in the manner pointed out. Thus to clairvoyant perception the earthly life of Christ is proved without any historical records.

One could think that Christ had said, 'I will be such an ideal for you human beings as, raised to a spiritual level, I will show you that which is otherwise fulfilled in each human body'. In his early childhood man learns from the spirit how to walk physically, i.e. he is shown by the spirit his *way* through earthly life. From the spirit he learns to speak, i.e. to form *truth;* in other words, he develops the essence of truth out of sound during the first three years of his life. And the *life* too which man lives on Earth as an ego-being obtains its life-organ through what is formed in the first three years. Thus man learns to walk, to find the way, he learns to present truth through his organism, and he learns to bring life from the spirit into expression in his body. No more significant reinterpretation seems thinkable of the words 'Except ye become as little children ye cannot enter into the kingdom of heaven'. And momentous is that saying in which the ego-being of Christ comes to expression thus: 'I am the Way, the Truth and the Life'. Just as, unknown to the child, the higher spirit forces are fashioning its organism to become the bodily expression of the way, the truth and the life, so the spirit of man, through being interpenetrated with Christ, gradually becomes the *conscious* vehicle of the way, the truth and the life. Man thereby makes himself in the course of his earthly development into that force which bears sway within him as a child, when he is not consciously its vehicle.

This saying about the way, the truth and the life is capable of

opening the doors of eternity. It sounds to man out of the depths
of his soul, if his self-knowledge is true and real.

3. TWO PATHS TO CHRIST TODAY

Those who strive along the path of spiritual science are specially
moved to ask in earnest: How do I find the true way to that unique
divine being who may rightly be called Christ? Merely through
being born and living with a life of soul which follows the customary development from birth to death, we have no inducement
to come to Christ, however spiritual we may be. . .

The initiative to take the way to Christ, even though it be often
an impulse rising from an obscure feeling, must come out of ourselves. . . Anyone who has developed normally and healthily cannot deny God, for it is ludicrous to believe that the healthy human
organism can have other than a divine origin. . . But that gener-
alized divinity, which out of inner falsehood is often called Christ
by modern pastors, is not Christ.

We come to Christ only — and here I refer to the immediate
present — if we go beyond the customary conditions of health
given by nature. For the Mystery of Golgotha was enacted on Earth
because mankind would not have been able to maintain a worthy
human status without it. And so we must not merely discover our
human nature between birth and death: we must rediscover it, if
we are to be Christians in a true sense, able to draw near Christ.
We must nerve ourselves to the inner honesty to say: 'Since the
Mystery of Golgotha we have not been born free from prejudice
in our world of thought; we are all born with certain prejudices'.
Freedom from prejudice in my thinking is something I have to
achieve during my life. And how can I achieve it? The one and only
way is this: instead of taking an interest merely in what I myself
think, and in what *I* consider right, I must develop a selfless interest
in every opinion I encounter, however strongly I may hold it to
be mistaken. The more a man prides himself on his dogmatic opinions and is interested only in them, the further he removes himself, at this moment of evolution, from Christ. The more he
develops a social interest in the opinions of other men, even though
he considers them erroneous, the more light he receives into his
own thinking from the opinions of others, the more he does to

fulfil in his inmost soul a saying of Christ which today must be interpreted in the sense of the new Christ-language.

Christ said: 'Inasmuch as ye have done it unto one of the least of these my brethren, ye have done it unto me'. Christ never ceases to reveal Himself anew to men — even unto the end of earthly time! And thus He says today to those willing to listen: 'In whatever the least of your brethren thinks, you must recognize that I am thinking in him; and that I enter into your feeling, whenever you bring another's thought into relation with your own, whenever you feel a fraternal interest for what is passing in another's soul. Whatever opinion, whatever outlook on life, you discover in the least of your brethren, therein you are seeking Myself'. So does Christ, Who desires to reveal Himself in a new way to men of the twentieth century, speak to our life of thought... If I do not look on myself alone as the source of everything I think, but recognize myself, right down to the depths of my soul, as a member of the human community, then, my dear friends, one way to Christ lies open. This must be characterized as *the way to Christ through thinking*. Earnest self-training so that we gain a true perception for estimating the thoughts of others, and for correcting bias in ourselves — this we must take as one of life's serious tasks.

The other way is through the will. Here too people are much addicted to a false way. Youth still keeps some idealism, but humanity today is dry and matter-of-fact, proud of what is often called practicality but is only a certain narrowness. Humanity today has no use for ideals drawn from the fountain of the spirit. Youth still has these ideals. Never was the life of older people so different from the life of the young as it is today. Lack of understanding among human beings is everywhere the great mark of our time... We may try to understand youth through its idealism; that is all very well, but today efforts are made to drive this idealism out of young people by depriving them of the imaginative education which is given by legends and fairy tales, by all that leads away from dry external perceptions. It will not be too easy, all the same, to drive all the youthful, natural, original idealism out of young people! But what is this? It is a great, a beautiful thing, but it ought not to be all-sufficient; for it is in fact bound up with the *Ex Deo Nascimur*, with the Jehovah aspect of the divine; and that is just what must not remain sufficient, now that the Mystery of Golgotha has been enacted on Earth.

Something further is required: idealism must spring from inner development, from self-education. We must see to it that something else is achieved, precisely an *achieved idealism*: not merely idealism that springs from the instincts and enthusiasm of youth, but one that is nurtured, gained by one's own initiative. Self-acquired initiative will not fade away with the passing of youth, it opens the way to Christ because again it is acquired during the life between birth and death. Feel the great difference between youthful idealism and that which springs from taking hold of the life of the spirit and can be ever and again kindled anew, because we have made it part of our soul independently of bodily existence. This is *the way to Christ through willing*.

Do not ask for abstract ways to Christ; ask for concrete ways! If you cultivate this idealism, or introduce it into the education of young people, you will have something which inspires men not only to do what the outer world impels them to do but to do more, to act out of the spirit. We then act in accordance with the intentions of Christ, Who did not descend from worlds above the Earth merely to achieve earthly ends, but in order to realize the super-earthly. We shall grow together with Him only if we cultivate idealism in ourselves, so that Christ, who represents the super-earthly within the Earth, can work through us. Only in achieved idealism can there be realized the intention of the saying of Paul about Christ: 'Not I, but Christ in me'.

These are the two ways through which we can find Christ. If we pursue them, we shall speak of Christ as the divine power active in our rebirth, while Jehovah is the divine power active in our birth. People must today learn to make this distinction, for this alone leads to genuine social feeling, genuine interest in our fellow men. Whoever develops an achieved idealism in himself will also have love for human-kind... You can keep on preaching love, love, love: that is mere sermonizing, mere words. Strive rather that men should experience a rebirth of idealism, an idealism which persists throughout life; then you will kindle in the soul the love of man for man, and be led out of egoism towards an objective concern for others.

And if you follow this twofold way to the renewal of Christianity, there is one thing you will certainly experience. Out of

thinking which is inwardly tolerant and interested in the thoughts
of others, and out of willing reborn through the achievement of
idealism, unfolds a heightened feeling of responsibility for every
action one performs. . . . This heightened feeling of responsibility
impels one to say: 'Can I justify this that I am doing or thinking,
not merely with reference to the immediate circumstances and
environment of my life, but in the light of my awareness of belonging to the supersensible spiritual world? Can I justify it in the light
of my knowledge that everything I do will be inscribed in an
akashic record of everlasting significance, where it will work on?
Oh, it comes powerfully home to one, this supersensible responsibility towards all things! It strikes one like a solemn warning,
when one seeks the twofold way to Christ — as though a being
stood behind one, looking over one's shoulder and saying repeatedly: "Thou art not responsible only to the world around thee,
but also to the divine-spiritual, for all thy thoughts and all thy
actions".'

But this being who looks over our shoulder, who heightens
and refines our sense of responsibility and sets us on a new path
— he is one who first directs us truly to Christ, Who went through
the Mystery of Golgotha. This Christ-way is most intimately
connected with the deepest social impulses and tasks of our
time.

4. BALANCE BETWEEN OPPOSING POWERS

When do we speak truly of spirit? We are justified in speaking of
the spirit only when we mean the spirit as *creator* of the material.
The worst kind of talk about the spirit — even though this talk
is often looked upon today as very beautiful — is that which treats
the spirit as though it dwelt in Utopia, as if this spirit should not
be touched at all by the material. No; when we speak of the spirit,
we must mean the spirit that has the power to plunge down directly
into the material. And when we speak of spiritual science, this must
be conceived as not merely rising above nature, but as being at
the same time valid natural science. We must mean the spirit with
which the human being can so unite himself as to enable this spirit,
through man's meditation, to weave itself even into the social life.
A spirit of which one speaks only in a drawing room, which one

would like to please by goodness and brotherly love, but a spirit that has no intention of immersing itself in our everyday life — such a spirit is not the true spirit, but a human abstraction; and worship of such a spirit is not worship of the real spirit, but is precisely the final emanation of materialism...

We have in modern consciousness the feeling of a contrast between heaven and hell; others call it spirit and matter. Fundamentally there are differences only of degree between the heaven and hell of the peasant and the matter and spirit of the philosophers of our day. The actual contrast is between God and devil, between paradise and hell. People are certain that paradise is good, and it is dreadful that men have left it; paradise is something that is lost; it must be sought again; and the devil is a terrible adversary who opposes all those powers connected with the concept of paradise... People have gradually dreamed themselves into this contrast, not knowing that striving towards this condition of paradise is just as bad for man, if he intends to have it forthwith, as striving for the opposite would be. For, if our concept of the structure of the world resembles that which underlies Milton's *Paradise Lost*, then we change the name of a power harmful to humanity when it is sought one-sidedly, to that of a divinely good power; and we oppose to it a contrast that is not a true contrast: namely, the devil, that in human nature resists the good.

The protest against this view is to be expressed in that sculptured group which is to be erected in the east part of our building, a group 9½m high in wood, by means of which, instead of the contrast between God and the devil, there is placed what must form the basis of the human consciousness of the future: the trinity consisting of the Luciferic, of what pertains to Christ, and of the Ahrimanic... Man must recognize that his true nature can be expressed only by the picture of *equilibrium* — that on the one side he is tempted to soar beyond his head, as it were, to soar into the fantastic, the ecstatic, the falsely mystical, into all that is fanciful: that is the one power. The other is that which draws man down into the materialistic, into the prosaic, the arid, and so on. We understand man only when we perceive him, in accordance with his nature, as striving for balance between the Luciferic on one arm of the scales, let us say, and on the other the Ahrimanic. Man has constantly to strive for the state of balance between these two powers: the one which would like to lead him out beyond himself, and the other tending to drag him down beneath himself. Now modern spiritual civilization has confused the fantastic, the ecstatic quality of the Luciferic, with the divine; so that in what is described as paradise, actually the description of the Luciferic is presented, and the frightful error is committed of confusing the Luciferic and the divine — because it is not understood that the thing of importance is to preserve the state of balance between the two powers pulling us toward the one side or the other.

This fact had first to be brought to light. If we are to strive toward what is Christian we must know clearly that this effort can be made only at the point of balance between the Luciferic and the Ahrimanic; and that especially the last three or four centuries have so largely eliminated knowledge of the real human being that little is known of this equilibrium. The Luciferic has been renamed the divine in *Paradise Lost*, and a contrast is made between it and that which is no longer Ahriman but has become the modern devil, or matter, or something of the kind.

Thus emphatically must we call attention to the spirit of modern civilization, because it is necessary for humanity to understand clearly how it has come upon a declivitous path, and can again begin to ascend only through the most radical corrective. People today would like to escape from the Earth environment by means of a 'spiritual' view. They do not know that when man flees into an abstract spiritual kingdom, he does not find the spirit at all, but the Luciferic kingdom. And much that today calls itself mysticism or theosophy is a quest for the Luciferic region. For mere knowledge of the spirit cannot form the basis of man's present day spiritual striving. . .

Especially when we direct our gaze toward spritual worlds should the question concern us: Why are we born out of the spiritual worlds into this physical world? Because here on Earth there are things to be learned, to be experienced, which cannot be experienced in the spiritual worlds; in order to experience these things we must descend into this physical world, and from this physical world carry up into the spiritual worlds the results of this experience. To do that we must really plunge into this physical world. For the sake of the spiritual world we must immerse ourselves in this physical world.

5. THE NATURE OF LOVE

Suppose we work, and earn by it; it may also be the case that our work brings us no joy, because we do it to pay off debts, not for reward. We may imagine that we have already spent what we now earn; we would prefer to have no debts, but must work to pay them off. Now let us apply this to our actions in general. In everything we do out of love, we pay off debts! Seen esoterically, what is done out of love brings no reward, but compensates for value already expended. The only actions from which we gain nothing in future are those we perform out of true, genuine love. This truth may come as a shock, and men are lucky to know nothing of it in their upper consciousness. But in their subconsciousness everyone knows it, and that is why deeds of love are done so unwillingly, why there is so little love in the world. Men feel instinctively that they may expect nothing in future for their 'I' from deeds of love. An advanced stage of development must have been reached before the soul can enjoy performing deeds of love, from which nothing is to be gained for itself. The impulse for this is not strong in humanity, but esotericism can be a source of powerful incentives to deeds of love.

Our egoism gains nothing from deeds of love, but the world gains all the more. Love is for the world what the Sun is for outer life. No soul could live if love departed from the world; it is the moral Sun of the world. Would it not be absurd if a man who delights in flowers were to wish that the Sun would vanish from the world? In terms of moral life, this means that it must be our concern that an impulse for sound development shall penetrate the affairs of humanity. To spread love over the Earth to the greatest degree possible, to promote love — that alone is wisdom.

What do we learn from spiritual science? We experience the Earth's evolution, we hear of the Spirit of the Earth, of the changing conditions of the Earth's surface, of the development of the human body, and so forth; we learn to know precisely what lives and weaves in evolution. When people do not want to know anything about spiritual science, it means that they have no interest for what is reality; for if a man does not want to know about Ancient Saturn, Ancient Sun, Ancient Moon,* then he can know

*See Chapter 2.2 — *Levels of Consciousness.*

nothing about the Earth. This lack of interest in the world is egoism in its grossest form. Interest in all existence is the duty of man. Let us long for and love the sun, with its creative power, its love for the wellbeing of the earth and the souls of men! This interest in the earth's evolution should be the spiritual seed of love for the world; for spiritual science without love would be a danger to mankind. But love should not be preached; it must and will come into the world through the spreading of knowledge of spiritual realities.

Love mediated by the senses is the wellspring of creative power, of that which is coming into being. Without sense-born love, the material would no longer exist in the world; without spiritual love, nothing spiritual can arise in evolution. When we practise love, cultivate love, *creative forces* pour into the world. Is the intellect to offer reasons for this? The creative forces must have poured into the world before we and our intellect came into being. True, we can as egoists deprive the future of creative forces; but we cannot obliterate the deeds of love and the creative forces of the past. To them we owe our existence. The strength we have from them is the measure of our debt to the past, and whatever love we may bring forth is payment of debts owed for our existence. From this we can understand the deeds of a highly developed person, for he has still greater debts. His wisdom lies in paying off his debts through deeds of love. The impulse of love grows with higher development; wisdom alone does not suffice. . . We have to leave our deeds of love behind in the world, where they are inscribed into the spiritual world process. It is through deeds of a different character that we perfect ourselves; for our deeds of love it is the world that is richer. For love is the creative element in the world.

Besides love there are two other powers in the world — might and wisdom. We can speak of weaker, stronger or absolute might, omnipotence; the same applies to wisdom. . . but the concept of enhancement cannot rightly be applied to love. Can omnipotence be ascribed to the divine being who lives and weaves through the world? Prejudices born of feeling must here be silent: were God omnipotent, He would be responsible for everything that happens, and there could be no human freedom! If man can be free, then certainly divine omnipotence is not present. Is the Godhead omniscient? As likeness to God is man's highest goal, we must strive towards omniscience. But if it is the supreme treasure, a vast chasm must yawn at every moment between man and God, of which man must always be aware if God had this supreme treasure and withheld it from man. The most all-encompassing attribute of God is neither omnipotence nor omniscience, but it is *love*, the attribute of which no enhancement is possible. God is uttermost love, unalloyed love, is born as it were out of the substance of love. God is pure love, not supreme wisdom, not supreme might. God has retained love for Himself, but has shared wisdom with Lucifer and might with Ahriman, in order that man may become free, in order that under the influence of wisdom he may perfect himself.

Love is the foundation of whatever is creative. Progress is attained through wisdom and strength. We see in the progress of humanity how the development of wisdom and strength changes, there is progressive evolution. Then the impulse of Christ poured at one time into mankind through the mystery of Golgotha. Love did not come into the world by degrees, it streamed into mankind as a gift of the Godhead in complete, perfect wholeness. But man can receive its impulse gradually into himself. . . Love wakens no expectations in the future, being payment of debts incurred in the past. And such was the Mystery of Golgotha in the world's evolution. Did the Godhead, then, owe any debt to humanity?

Lucifer's influence brought into humanity a certain element, in consequence of which something man previously possessed was withdrawn from him. This new element led to a descent that was countered by the Mystery of Golgotha, which made possible the payment of all debts. The impulse of Golgotha did not come in order that the sins we have committed in evolution may be removed from us, but that what crept into humanity through Lucifer should be given its counterweight.

Let us imagine that there is a man who knows nothing of the name of Jesus Christ, nothing of what is communicated in the Gospels, but that he understands the radical difference between the nature of wisdom and might and that of love. Such a man, even though he knows nothing of the Mystery of Golgotha, is a Christian in the truest sense. . .

May God's grace-bringing guardian ray
Brim-over my expanding soul,
That it may apprehend
Strength-giving forces everywhere.
This then its solemn vow:
To wake the might of love
Within it to full life,
Beholding thus God's power
Upon its path of life,
Working as God would work
With everything it has.

COMING EVENTS

1. MICHAEL AND THE NEW CHRIST-CONSCIOUSNESS

Just as in Ancient Hebrew times, which were a direct preparation for the Mystery of Golgotha, the Hebrew initiates could turn to Michael as the outer revelation of Jehovah, so we are now in a position to turn to Michael — who from being the messenger of Jehovah has now become the messenger of Christ — in order to receive from him during the next few centuries increasing spiritual revelation that will unveil to us the Mystery of Golgotha more and more. That which happened 2000 years ago, but could only be made known through the various Christian denominations, and the depths of which can only be unveiled in the twentieth century, when instead of science spiritual knowledge (our gift from Michael) comes into play — it is that which should fill our hearts with unfathomably deep feelings in our present time. Within the last few decades a door has opened through which understanding can come to us.

Michael can give us new spiritual light, which we may look on as a transformation of that light given through him at the time of the Mystery of Golgotha; and men of our time may place themselves in this light. If we can sense this we can grasp the whole significance of the new age that is to come within the next few centuries. Indeed, because humanity has become freer than in former times, we shall through our own wills be able to progress so far as to receive this revelation.

We may now refer to the event in the higher worlds which has led to this altered state of affairs. We remind ourselves of that which may often have streamed into our souls through what occurred at the baptism of John in Jordan, when Christ revealed himself in human form, visible upon Earth among mankind. Let us further fill our souls with the thought of how Christ then, as regards his outward form, joined the Hierarchy of the Angels, and has since that time lived invisibly in the Earth sphere. Now in the invisible worlds there is no death. Christ Himself, because He descended into our world, went through a death similar to that of men, and when He once more became a purely spiritual being He still retained the memory of His death. But as a being of the rank of the Angels in which he manifests Himself further outwardly, He could experience only a diminution of consciousness.

Through the triumph of science since the sixteenth century. . . materialistic and agnostic sentiments of greater intensity than hitherto came into mankind. As men passed up to the spiritual worlds through the gate of death, they increasingly took with them the results of their materialistic ideas, so that after the sixteenth century more and more seeds of earthly materialism were carried over, which developed in a special way. The Angel which was the outer form of Christ since that time suffered in the course of the nineteenth century an extinction of consciousness as the result of the materialistic opposing forces that had come up to the spiritual worlds. And the entry of unconsciousness into the spiritual worlds in this way will in the twentieth century become the resurrection of Christ-consciousness within the souls of mankind on Earth between birth and death. Hence one may foretell that in a certain sense what has been lost by mankind as consciousness will certainly again arise for clairvoyant vision from the twentieth century onwards. At first only a few and then an ever-increasing number of people in this twentieth century will be able to perceive the appearance of the etheric Christ, that is to say, Christ in the form of an Angel. . .*

Thus Christ-consciousness can be united with the earthly consciousness of mankind from the twentieth century onwards; for the dying of the Christ-consciousness in the angelic sphere in the

*Steiner speaks here of the 'appearing' (epiphaneia). Two further stages mentioned in the New Testament need to be distinguished: 'revelation' (apokalypsis) and 'coming' (parousia). The 'second coming' is more gradual than usually supposed.

nineteenth century signifies the resurrection of the *direct* Christ-consciousness in the earthly sphere — that is to say, the life of Christ will be felt as a direct personal experience in the souls of men. Just as the few who could then read the signs of the times were able so to look upon the Mystery of Golgotha as to realize that this great, mighty Being descended to live on Earth and go through death in order that the substances of His being might thereby be embodied in the Earth, so are *we* able to perceive that in worlds lying immediately behind our own a sort of spiritual death, a suspension of consciousness and thereby a repetition of the Mystery of Golgotha took place, in order that a revival of the formerly concealed Christ-consciousness can take place within the souls of men on Earth... Twice already has Christ been crucified; once physically in the physical world at the beginning of our era, and a second time in the nineteenth century, spiritually, as described. One might say that mankind experienced the resurrection of His body in that former time; it will experience the resurrection of His *consciousness* from the twentieth century onwards.

That which I have only been able to indicate in a few words will gradually enter men's souls, and the mediator, the messenger, will be Michael, who is now the envoy of Christ. Just as he formerly guided men's souls to understand the directing of His life from heaven to Earth, so is he now preparing mankind that it may be able to experience the directing of the Christ-consciousness from the unknown into the known. And just as then most of His contemporaries were unable to believe what a mighty thing had happened in the evolution of the Earth, so in our day those in the world at large strive to increase the power of materialism, and will continue for a long time to consider what has been spoken of today as phantasy, dreaming, perhaps even folly. And thus too will they consider this truth concerning Michael, who is now beginning to reveal Christ anew. Nevertheless many people will recognize that which is now commencing like a new dawn, and which during coming centuries will pour itself into human souls like a sun — for Michael may always be likened to a sun. And even if many people fail to recognize this new Michael-revelation, nevertheless it will spread over humanity...

2. THE ETHERIC CHRIST

At the time when Jesus Christ lived on Earth, imminent events were rightly understood by those who came to his forerunner John, and were baptized by him in the way described in the Gospels. They received baptism so that their sins, that is, the karma of their previous lives which had ended, might be changed, and that they might realize that the most important Impulse for earthly evolution would descend at this time into a physical body. But human evolution goes on, and in our present age it is important that people should learn to accept the knowledge of spiritual science, and should be able gradually so to fire what streams from their *hearts* to the brain that it can meet anthroposophy with understanding.

The result of this will be that people will be able to receive and comprehend that which begins in the twentieth century: this is the etheric Christ, in contrast to the physical Christ of Palestine. For we have reached the point of time when the etheric Christ enters the life of the Earth, and will become visible, at first to a few people, through a kind of natural clairvoyance. Then in the course of the next three thousand years He will become visible to ever more people. This must come to pass; it is a natural event. That it will happen is just as certain as that the achievements of electricity have happened in the nineteenth century. It is true that a certain number of people will see the etheric Christ, and will experience the event that took place before Damascus; but this will depend on their learning to watch for the moment when Christ draws near to them. In a few decades* it will happen to certain people, especially the young — for it is already in preparation — that someone arrives in a place and experiences certain things. Then if he has really sharpened his vision through occupying himself with anthroposophy, he will notice that suddenly someone is beside him, Who comes to help him, to draw his attention to this or that: that Christ approaches him, but he thinks a physical man is there. Then he will notice that it is a supersensible Being, Who suddenly disappears. Many a one will experience, when sitting silent in his room, his heart sad and oppressed, not knowing which way to turn, that the door will open: the etheric Christ will appear and speak comforting words to him. Christ

*This was spoken in 1911.

will become a living comforter to men. However grotesque it may seem today, yet it is true that many a time, when people are sitting together not knowing what to do, and also when a greater number of people are waiting expectantly, they will then behold the etheric Christ. He will Himself be there, and will confer with them, will contribute His voice to such gatherings. These times are now approaching. This is something which as a positive constructive element is entering human evolution...

3. THE LORD OF KARMA

Until now there were only two sources of knowledge concerning the Christian mysteries for those who could not rise through training to clairvoyant observation. One was the Gospels, all that comes from the communications contained in them or in the traditions connected with them. The second arose because there have always been clairvoyant individuals who could see into the higher worlds, and who through their own knowledge brought down the facts of the event of Christ; other persons followed these individuals, receiving from them a never-ending Gospel, as it were, which could continually come into the world through those who were clairvoyant... And now from the twentieth century onward a third source begins. It arises because an ever-increasing number of persons will experience an extension, an enhancement of the forces of cognition which is *not* brought about through meditation, concentration and other exercises. More and more people will be able to renew for themselves the event of Paul on the way to Damascus. Thereby a period will begin of which we can say that it will provide a direct means of perceiving the significance and the being of Christ Jesus...

Just as we must say that for Christ Himself, the event of Golgotha had the significance that with this very event a God died, a God overcame death — the deed had not happened before, and it is now an accomplished fact — so will an event of profound significance take place, not however on the physical plane but in the etheric world. And through the fact that this event connected with Christ Himself takes place, the possibility will be created for men to learn to see Christ, to look upon Him. What is this event?

This event is none other than that a certain function in the cosmos connected with the evolution of humanity passes over to Christ in the twentieth century, in a more enhanced manner than has so far been the case. In our age the important event takes place that Christ becomes the Lord of Karma for human evolution. This is the beginning of that which we also find in the New Testament (Acts 10.42: 'He is the one ordained by God to be Judge of the living and the dead'*). But according to esoteric research this event is not to be understood as though it were a single event which takes place once on the physical plane; rather is it connected with the whole evolution of humanity. And whereas Christian evolution so far signifies a kind of preparation, there now happens the significant fact that Christ becomes the Lord of Karma, that in the future it will rest with Him to decide what our karmic account is, how our credit and debit in life stand to one another.†

What is now being said has been a matter of general knowledge in Western occultism for many centuries, and is denied by no occultist who knows these things. But specially of late it has been again newly established with utmost care. . .

Now there are a great many men, especially such as have gone through the development of Western civilization —. these things are not the same for all peoples — who experience a quite definite fact in the moment following the separation of the etheric body after death. We know that for men the passing through the gate of death is such that we separate ourselves from the physical body. The individual is at first still connected for a time with his etheric body, but afterwards he separates his astral body and ego from the etheric body. He takes with him an extract of this etheric body, and the chief part of it goes another way; it usually becomes part of the general cosmic ether, either dissolving completely — this is only the case in imperfect conditions — or continuing to work on as a closed form of consequences. When the individual has stripped off his etheric body he passes over into the region of kamaloca for the period of purification in the soul world. But before this a quite special experience takes place. . . The individual experiences the meeting with a quite definite being, who presents him with his karmic account; and this individuality who stands there as a kind of accountant of the karmic powers had for a great

*Also 2 Tim 4.1: 'Christ Jesus who is to judge the living and the dead'.
†See Chapter 4.1 — *Practical Workings of Karma.*

number of men the form of Moses. Hence the mediaeval formula which originated in Rosicrucianism: Moses presents man in the hour of his death — the expression is not quite accurate, but that is immaterial here — with the register of his sins, and at the same time points to the 'stern law'. Thus the man can recognize how he has departed from this stern law according to which he ought to have acted.

This function passes over in the course of our time — and this is the signficant point — to Christ Jesus; and man will ever more and more meet Christ Jesus as his Judge, as his karmic Judge. That is the supersensible event. Exactly in the same way as on the physical plane at the beginning of our era the event of Palestine took place, so does the transference of the function of karmic Judge to Christ Jesus take place in our time in the next higher world. This fact so works into the physical world that man will develop regarding it the *feeling* that by everything he does, he is causing something for which he will be accountable to the judgement of Christ. This feeling, which is appearing now quite naturally in the course of human development, will be transformed so that it impregnates the soul with a light which gradually shines out from the individual himself, and *will illuminate the form of Christ* within the etheric world. And the more this feeling is developed — a feeling that will have more enhanced significance than the abstract conscience — the more will the etheric form of Christ be visible in the coming centuries. This fact we shall have to characterize more exactly in the following lectures. . .

Men of the future will increasingly feel: I am going through the gate of death with my karmic account. On the one side stand my good, clever and beautiful deeds, my good, clever, beautiful and intelligent thoughts; on the other side stands everything evil, wicked, stupid, foolish and loathsome. But He who will in future, for the incarnations which will follow in human evolution, have the function of Judge to bring order into this karmic account, is Christ! We have actually to imagine this to ourselves as follows.

After we have gone through the gate of death we shall be incarnated again in a later period. Events will have to happen for us through which our karma can be balanced, for every person must reap what he has sown. Karma remains a righteous law. But what the karmic law has to fulfil is not only there for individual men. Karma does not only balance the egoism, but in the case of each individual the balancing must take place so that in the best possible way the karmic account fits in with the general affairs of the whole world. We must so balance our karma that we can help forward in the best possible manner the progress of the whole human race on Earth. For this we need enlightenment, not only the general knowledge that the karmic fulfilment of our deeds must take place. Karmic fulfilment which can compensate for a deed may be of this or that nature. But because one way of fulfilment would be more serviceable for the general progress of humanity than another, we must choose those thoughts, feelings or sensations which pay off our karma, and at the same time serve the collective progress of humanity. It falls in future to Christ to bring the balance of our karma into line with general Earth karma, the general progress of humanity. And it happens principally in the time in which we live between death and a new birth. But it will also be prepared in the epoch we are approaching, before the doors of which we now stand, in such a way that in the event man will acquire more and more the capacity for having a special experience. Today only a very few have it, but continually more and more persons will from the middle of this century onwards through the next thousand years have the following experience.

The person in question has done this or that. He will bethink himself, will have to gaze on what he has done, and something like a dream-picture will rise up before him which will make a quite remarkable impression on him. He will say to himself: I cannot recall that it is a remembrance of something that I have done, but yet it is as if it were an experience of mine. Like a dream-picture it will stand there before him, closely concerned with him; but he cannot recall that he has experienced or done it in the past. If he is an anthroposopher he will understand the matter, otherwise he will have to wait until he comes to anthroposophy and learns to understand it. The anthroposopher will know: what you see there as a consequence of your deed is a picture of what will happen to you in the future; the balancing of your deed appears to you in advance. The epoch is beginning in which men, in the moment in which they have committed a deed, will have a premonition, a feeling, perhaps even a clear picture of the way this deed will be balanced by karma.

Thus in closest connection with human experience, enhanced capacities will arise for humanity in the next epoch. These will be mighty incentives to morality, and will signify something quite different from the voice of conscience, which has been the preparation for these impulses. The individual will no longer believe that what you have done is something that can die with you. But he will know quite exactly: The act will not die with you; as an act it will have a consequence which will live further with you. And many another thing will the individual know. The time in which men closed the doors to the spiritual world is approaching its end. Men must again climb upwards to the spiritual world. The capacities will so awaken that men will be partakers of the spiritual world.

Clairvoyance will always be something different from this participation. Just as there was an ancient clairvoyance that was dreamlike, so there will be a future clairvoyance that is not dreamlike, through which people will know what they have done, and what it signifies. Something else will also come about. The individual will know: I am not alone; everywhere live spiritual beings who stand in relationship to me. And men will learn to communicate with these beings, and to live amongst them. And in the next three thousand years that which we may call the karmic Judgeship of Christ will appear as a truth to a sufficiently large number of persons. Men will experience Christ as an etheric form. They will so experience Him that, like Paul before Damascus, they will know quite intimately that Christ lives.

4. THE MISSION OF THE EARTH

Complicated processes were connected with Jesus of Nazareth in order that for three years the impulse of Christ might live within him.* Even then Christ was not 'incarnated' in the ordinary sense, but 'pervaded' the body of Jesus of Nazareth. This must be understood when it is said that it is not possible to speak of a 'return' of Christ, but only of an impulse which was present *once* during the events beginning with the Baptism. Christ was then present

*See Steiner's lectures on *The Gospel of St Luke.*

on the very soil of the Earth. From that time Christ has been united
with the spiritual atmosphere of the Earth, and can be found there
by souls willing to receive Him.

Even the outer senses discern that the Earth planet is in a process of pulverization, and will at some future time disintegrate
into dust. The Earth-body will be cast off by the spirit of the Earth,
as the human body is cast off by the individual human spirit. What
will remain as the highest substance of the Earth when its goal
has been reached? The impulse of Christ was present on Earth
as 'spiritual substance', and will be absorbed into men during the
course of Earth's evolution. But how does it live on? When Christ
was upon the Earth for three years He had no physical body, no
ether body, no astral body of His own, but was enveloped in the
three sheaths of Jesus of Nazareth. When the goal has been reached,
the Earth, like man, will be a fully-developed being, a meet and
fitting vehicle for the impulse of Christ.

But from whence are the three sheaths of this impulse of Christ
derived? From forces that can be unfolded only on the Earth.
Whatever has since that time unfolded on Earth as the power of
wonder, whatever comes to life in us as wonder, passes finally to
Christ, weaving the astral body of the Christ impulse. *Love* or
compassion in human souls weaves the ether body of the Christ
impulse. And the power of *conscience*, which lives in and inspires
the souls of men from the time of the Mystery of Golgotha until
the goal of the Earth is attained, weaves what corresponds with
the physical body for the Christ impulse.

The true meaning of words from the Gospel can only now
be discerned: 'Whatsoever you have done to one of the least of
these My brethren, ye have done it unto Me.' (Matthew 25.40).
The forces streaming from man to man are the units integrating
the ether body of Christ: love or compassion weaves the ether
body of Christ. Thus when the goal of Earth evolution is attained,
He will be enveloped in the threefold vesture woven from the
powers that have lived in men — and which, when the limita-
tions of the 'I' have been transcended, become the sheaths of
Christ.

Now think how men live in communion with Christ. Man
grows more perfect in that he develops as a being endowed with
the power of the 'I'. But men are united with Christ in that they

transcend their own 'I', and through wonder share in forming the astral body of Christ. His ether body will be fashioned through the compassion and love flowing from man to man, and his 'physical body' through the power of conscience unfolding in human beings. Whatever wrongs are committed in these three realms deprive Christ of the possibility of full development on the Earth — that is to say, Earth evolution is left imperfect, it cannot reach the goal of its evolution. The principle of egoism must be overcome in Earth evolution.

The attempts made hitherto do not even suggest what form a portrayal of Christ should take. For it would have to express how the enveloping sheaths woven of the forces of wonder, compassion and conscience are gradually made manifest. The countenance of Christ must be so vital and living that it expresses victory over the sensory, desire-nature in men — victory achieved through the very forces which have spiritualized the countenance. There must be sublime power in it. The painter or sculptor will have to express in the unusual form of the chin or mouth, the power of conscience unfolded to its highest degree. The mouth must convey the impression that it is not there for taking food, but to give utterance to whatever moral strength and power of conscience has been cultivated by men throughout the ages; the very structure of the bones around the teeth in the lower jaw will seem to form themselves into a mouth. The lower part of the face will have to express a power whose outstreaming rays seem to shatter the rest of the body to pieces, changing it in such a way that certain other forces are vanquished. On the other hand, all the power of compassion will flow out of His eyes — the power that eyes alone can contain — not in order to receive impressions, but to bear the very soul into the joys and sufferings of others. His brow will give no suggestion of thought based upon earthly sense-impressions. It will be a brow conspicuously prominent above the eyes, arching over that part of the brain; not a 'thinker's brow' which merely works on material already there. Wonder will be made manifest in this projecting brow which curves gently backwards over the head, expressing wonder and marvel at the mysteries of the world. It will be a head such as is nowhere to be found in physical humanity.

Every true representation of Christ must be a portrayal of the ideal embodied in Him. When man reaches out towards this highest ideal and strives through spiritual science to represent it in art, this feeling will arise in greater and greater strength: if you would portray Christ, you must not look at what is actually there in the world, but you must let your whole being be pervaded and quickened by all that flows from contemplation of the spiritual evolution of the world, inspired by the three great impulses of wonder, compassion and conscience.

5. THE DIVISION IN MANKIND

We have now reached a point in human evolution — all that I am saying now is in accordance with the presentation in the Apocalypse — when in a certain way mankind is confronted by the need for a decision. In our age an enormous amount of spiritual energy is used to provide for the lowest needs; telephone, telegraph, railway, liners, and other things still to come have absorbed and will absorb a tremendous amount of spiritual force; and they are only used for the mere satisfaction of lower human needs. Man, however, has only a certain amount of spiritual force. . . This had to be so; it would have gone badly with mankind if this had not come about. This spiritual power has also been used for many other things. Only consider how all social connections have gradually been spun into an extremely fine intellectual web. What spiritual forces have been expended so that one may draw a cheque in America and cash it in Japan! These forces had, so to speak, to descend below the line of the physical plane which separates the spiritual kingdom from the abyss. For in a certain way man has actually descended into the abyss, and one who studies the age from the standpoint of spiritual science can see by the most mundane phenomena how this progresses from decade to decade, how a certain point is always reached where the personality can still keep a hold on itself, how if at this point the personality allows itself to sink down it is lost, it is not rescued to be lifted into the spiritual worlds.

This may be illustrated by the most mundane things, for example in the details of the development of the banking system in the second half of the nineteenth century. Perhaps it is only for future historians to show clearly that a fundamental change then came about, which we may describe by saying that in banking affairs the personality was gradually shattered. I should have to draw your attention to the time when the four Rothschilds went out into the world from Frankfurt, one to Vienna, another to Naples, the third to London, the fourth to Paris. The whole banking system was thus brought into a personal sphere by the personal talent directed to it. The personality immersed itself in finance. Today you see banking affairs becoming impersonal. Capital passes into the hands of joint stock companies; it is no longer managed by the individual personality. Capital begins to control.★ Purely objective forces are at work in capital, and there are already forces in this realm which draw all the will of the personality to themselves, so that the personality becomes powerless. Thus with seeing eyes one can penetrate these mundane things, and one can see everywhere how mankind has descended, as regards the personality, to the lowest depths.

Now the personality may save itself and ascend again. It can save itself, for example, by really learning to strengthen its inner soul-forces and depend upon itself, and make itself independent of the forces of capital. But the personality may also cast itself into these forces, it may in a certain way sail into and plunge into the abyss, by allowing itself to be ensnared by the forces active in capital.

The most important point of time, when the human personality descends as far as the Earth and has to turn back again, is that of the appearance of Christ Jesus on Earth. He gave to the Earth the power which made it possible for man to rise again; and man rises to the extent to which he has fellowship with Christ Jesus. To the extent that for a large part of mankind the understanding will dawn for what this event signified, so that for a large part of mankind this impulse of Christ becomes the innermost impulse of man's being, from which he works and weaves his existence, to this extent will mankind ascend again. Men must learn to understand more and more what St Paul said: 'It is not I who work; but Christ works in me'.

Therefore if this impulse enters livingly into the hearts of men and becomes the impulse behind their activity, then the ascent takes place; and all the souls which find this union with the prin-
★See further Chapter 7.3 — *Capital and Credit.*

ciple of Christ find the way upward. But all the souls who fail
to find this union would have gradually to go down into the abyss.
They would have gained the ego; they would have attained egoism, but would not be in a position to rise up again with this ego
into the spiritual world. And the consequence for a man who
makes no connection with the Christ-principle would be that he
disconnects himself from the spiritual ascent; instead of ascending he would descend and harden himself more and more in his
ego. Instead of having found in matter just the opportunity to
develop the ego and then rise up again, he would only descend
deeper and deeper into matter.

Yes, everything echoes. The possibility arose for man to enter
our physical world. By surviving the Atlantean flood it became
possible for him to create and develop his present human countenance, which is really an image of the spiritual ego-divinity
dwelling in man. . . Let us suppose a man were to deny that it
was the spirit which has given him the human countenance; then
he would not use the body as an opportunity to attain to
ego-consciousness and again spiritualize himself; but he would
grow together with the body and love it so much that he would
only feel at home in it. He would remain united with the body
and go down into the abyss. And because of not having used the
power of the spirit, the external shape would again come to resemble the previous form. The man who descends into the abyss would
become animal like.

Thus those who use the life in the body for anything more
than an opportunity to gain ego-consciousness will descend into
the abyss and form the evil race. They have turned away from the
impulse of Christ Jesus, and out of the ugliness of their souls they
will again develop the animal form man possessed in former ages.
The evil race, with its savage impulses, will dwell in animal form
in the abyss. And when up above those who have spiritualized
themselves, who have received the Christ-principle, announce what
they have to say regarding their union with the name Christ Jesus,
here below in the abyss will sound forth names of blasphemy, the
desire to escape what appears as spiritual transformation.

A person who thinks superficially might say at this point: Yes,
but very many have lived who have experienced nothing of the
impulse of Christ; why should not these have partaken in the

impulse of Christ Jesus? This is objected from the materialistic side: Why should salvation only come with Christ Jesus? But man returns again and again, and the souls which lived in earlier times will return in new bodies after the event of Christ, so that there are none who could not participate in the event of Christ Jesus. Such an objection can only be made by one who does not believe in reincarnation.

Thus we see how the division takes place.

Life is akin to fire —
Both are filled with seeds of beneficent actions,
Both place before man a different longing.
That our fortune in life may lack bitter pain
Only he can wish who stupidly supposes
There could be fire without sacrifice of fuel.

REORDERING OF SOCIETY

1. REQUIREMENTS OF SPIRITUAL, SOCIAL AND ECONOMIC LIFE

In the social movement of the present day there is a great deal of talk about social organization but very little about social and unsocial human beings. Little regard is paid to that 'social question' which arises when one considers that the arrangements of society take their social or antisocial stamp from the people who work in them. Socialist thinkers expect to see in the control of the means of production by the community what will satisfy the needs of the wider population. They take for granted that under such control the co-operation between people must take a social form. They have seen that the industrial system of private capitalism has led to unsocial conditions. They think that if this industrial system were to disappear, the antisocial effects must also end.

Undoubtedly along with the modern capitalistic form of economy there have arisen social ills to the widest extent; but is this any proof that they are a *necessary consequence* of this economic system? An industrial system can of its own nature do nothing but put men into situations in life that enable them to produce goods for themselves or for others in a useful or a useless manner. The modern industrial system has brought the means of production into the power of individuals or groups of persons. The technical achievements could best be exploited by a concentration of economic power. So long as this power is employed only in the production of goods, its social effect is essentially different from when it trespasses on the fields of civil rights or spiritual culture. And it is this trespassing which in the course of the last few centuries has led to those social ills for whose abolition the modern social movement is pressing. He who is in possession of the means of production acquires economic domination over others. This has resulted in his allying himself with the forces helpful to him in administration and parliaments, through which he was able to procure positions of social advantage over those who were economically dependent on him; and which even in a democratic state bear in practice the character of rights. Similarly this economic domination has led to a monopolizing of the life of spiritual culture by those who held economic power.

Now the simplest thing *seems* to be to get rid of this economic predominance of individuals, and thereby to do away with their predominance in rights and spiritual culture as well. One arrives at this 'simplicity' of social conception when one fails to remember that the combination of technical and economic activity which modern life demands necessitates allowing the most fruitful expansion possible to individual initiative and personal worth within the business of economic life. The form which production must take under modern conditions makes this a necessity. The individual cannot make his abilities effective in business, if he is tied down in his work and decisions to the will of the community. However dazzling the thought of the individual producing not for himself but for society collectively, yet its justice within certain bounds should not hinder one from also recognizing the other truth, that society collectively is incapable of originating economic decisions that permit of being realized through individuals in the desirable way. Really practical thought, therefore, will not look to find the cure for social ills in a reshaping of economic life that would substitute communal for private management of the means of production. The endeavour should rather be to forestall the ills that can arise through management by individual initiative and personal worth, without impairing this management itself. This is only possible if the relations of civil rights amongst those engaged in industry are not influenced by the interests of economic life, and if that which should be done for people through the spiritual life is also independent of these interests.

Genuine interests of right can only spring up on a ground where the life of rights is separately cultivated, and where the *only* consideration will be what the rights of a matter are. When people proceed from such considerations to frame rules of right, the rules

thus made will take effect in economic life. Then it will not be
necessary to place a restriction on the individual acquiring economic power; for such power will only result in his rendering
economic achievements proportionate to his abilities, but not in
using this to obtain privileged rights. . . Only when rights are
ordered in a field where a business consideration cannot in any
way come into question, where business can procure no power
over this system of rights, will the two be able to work together
in such a way that men's sense of right will not be injured, nor
economic ability be turned from a blessing to a curse for the community as a whole.

When those who are economically powerful are in a position
to use their power to wrest privileged rights for themselves, then
among the economically weak there will grow up a corresponding
opposition to these privileges; and this opposition must as soon
as it has grown strong enough lead to revolutionary disturbances.
If the existence of a special province of rights makes it impossible for such privileged rights to arise, then disturbances of this
sort cannot occur. . . One will never really touch what is working up through the social movement to the surface of modern life,
until one brings about social conditions in which, alongside the
claims and interests of the economic life, those of rights can find
realization and satisfaction on their own independent basis.

In a similar manner must one approach the question of the
cultural life, and its connections with the life of civil rights and
of industrial economy. The course of the last few centuries has
been such that the cultural life itself has been cultivated under conditions which only allowed of its exercising to a limited extent
an independent influence upon political life — that of civil rights
— or upon economics. One of the most important branches of
spiritual culture, the whole manner of education, was shaped by
the interests of the civil power. The human being was taught and
trained according as state interests required; and state power was
reinforced by economic power. If anyone was to develop his capacities within the existing provisions for education, he had to do so
on the basis of such finances as his place in life provided. Those
spiritual forces that could find scope within the life of political
rights or of industry accordingly acquired the stamp of the latter.
Any *free* spiritual life had to forego all idea of carrying its results

into the sphere of the state, and could only do so in the economic sphere in so far as this remained outside the sphere of activities of the state. In industry, after all, the necessity is obvious for allowing the competent person to find scope, since all fruitful activity dies out if left solely under the control of the incompetent whom circumstances may have endowed with economic power. If the tendency common amongst socialist thinkers were carried out and economic life were administered after the fashion of the political and legal, then the culture of the free spiritual life would be forced to withdraw altogether from the public field.

But a spiritual life that has to develop apart from civil and industrial realities loses touch with life. It is forced to draw its content from sources that are not in live connection with these realities; and in course of time it works this substance up into a shape which runs on like a sort of animated abstraction alongside the actual realities, without having any practical effect on them. And so two different currents arise in spiritual life. . . Consider what conceptions of the mind, what religious ideals, what artistic interests form the inner life of the shopkeeper, the manufacturer, or the government official, apart from his daily practical life; and then consider what ideas are contained in those activities expressed in his bookkeeping, or for which he is trained by the education and instruction that prepares him for his profession. A gulf lies between the two currents of spiritual life. The gulf has grown all the wider in recent years because the mode of conception which in natural science is quite justified has become the standard of man's relation to reality. This mode of conception proceeds from the knowledge of laws in things and processes lying outside the field of human activity and influence, so that man is as it were a mere spectator of that which he grasps in the laws of nature. . .

A spiritual conception that penetrates to the being of *man* finds there motives for action which ethically are directly good; for the impulse to evil arises in man only because in his thoughts and sensations he silences the depths of his own nature. Hence social ideas arrived at through the spiritual conception here meant must by their very nature be ethical ideas as well. And not being drawn from thought alone but experienced in life, they have the strength to lay hold on the will and live on in action. For true spiritual conception, social thought and ethical thought flow into one. . .

This kind of spirit can, however, thrive only when its growth is completely independent of all authority except such as is derived directly from the spiritual life itself. Legal regulations by the civil state for the nurture of the spirit sap the strength of the forces of spiritual life, whereas a spiritual life left to its own inherent interests and impulses will reach out into everything that man performs in social life. . .

If the life of the spirit be a free one, evolved only from impulses within itself, then civil life will thrive in proportion as people are educated intelligently from living spiritual experience in the adjustment of their relationships of rights; and economic life will be fruitful in the measure in which men's spiritual nurture has developed their capacities for it. . .

Because the spirit at work in civil life and the round of industry is no longer one through which the spiritual life of the individual finds a channel, he sees himself in a social order which gives him, as individual, no scope civically nor economically. People who do not see this clearly will always object to a view of the social organism divided into three independently functioning systems of the cultural life, the rights state and the industrial economy, that such a differentiation would destroy the necessary unity of communal life. One must reply to them that this unity is destroying itself, in the effort to maintain itself intact. . . It is just in separation that they will turn to unity, whereas in an artificial unity they become estranged.

Many socialist thinkers will dismiss such an idea with the phrase that conditions of life worth striving for cannot be brought about by this organic membering of society, but only through a suitable economic organization. They overlook the fact that the men at work in their organization are endowed with wills. If one tells them so they will smile, for they regard it as self-evident. Yet they envisage a social structure in which this 'self-evident' fact is left out of account. Their economic organization is to be controlled by a communal will, which must be the resultant wills of the people in the organization. These individual wills can never find scope, if the communal will is derived entirely from the idea of economic organization. . .

Most people today still lack faith in the possibility of establishing a socially satisfying order of society based on individual wills, because such a faith cannot come from a spiritual life dependent on the life of the state and of the economy. The kind of spirit that develops not in freedom out of the life of the spirit itself but out of an external organization simply does not know what the potentialities of the spirit are. It looks round for something to direct it, not knowing how the spirit directs itself if only it can draw its strength from its own resources.

For the new shaping of the social order, goodwill is not the only thing needed. It needs also that courage which can be a match for the lack of faith in the spirit's power. A true spiritual conception can inspire this courage; for it feels able to bring forth ideas that not only serve to give the soul its inward orientation, but which in their very birth bring with them seeds of life's practical configuration. The will to go down into the deep places of the spirit can become a will so strong as to bear a part in everything that man performs. . .

The experiments now being made to solve the social question afford such unsatisfactory results because many people have not yet become able to see what the true gist of the problem is. They see it arise in economic regions, and look to economic institutions to provide the answer. They think they will find the solution in economic transformations. They fail to recognize that these transformations can only come about through forces released from within human nature itself in the uprising of a new spiritual life and life of rights in their own independent realms.

2. THE FUNDAMENTAL SOCIAL LAW

Briefly as the subject must be dealt with, there will always be some people whose feeling will lead them to recognize the truth of what it is impossible to discuss in all its fullness here.

There is a fundamental social law which spiritual science teaches, and which is as follows:

'The well-being of a community of people working together will be the greater, the less the individual claims for himself the proceeds of his work, i.e. the more of these proceeds he makes over to his fellow-workers, the more his own needs are satisfied, not out of his own work but out of the work done by others'.

Every arrangement in a community that is contrary to this law will inevitably engender somewhere after a while distress and want. It is a fundamental law, which holds good for all social life with the same absoluteness and necessity as any law of nature within a particular field of natural causation. It must not be supposed, however, that it is sufficient to acknowledge this law as one for general moral conduct, or to try to interpret it into the sentiment that everyone should work in the service of his fellow men. No, this law only lives in reality as it should when a community of people succeeds in creating arrangements such that no one *can* ever claim the fruits of his own labour for himself, but that these go wholly to the benefit of the community. And he must himself be supported in return by the labours of his fellow men. The important point is, therefore, that working for one's fellow men and obtaining so much income must be kept apart, as two separate things.

Self-styled 'practical people' will of course have nothing but a smile for such 'outrageous idealism'. And yet this law is more practical than any that was ever devised or enacted by the 'practicians'. Anyone who really examines practical life will find that every community that exists or has ever existed anywhere has two sorts of arrangements, of which the one is in accordance with this law and the other contrary to it. It is bound to be so everywhere, whether men will it or not. Every community would indeed fall to pieces at once, if the work of the individual did not pass over into the totality. But human egoism has from of old run counter to this law, and sought to extract as much as possible for the individual out of his own work. And what has come about from of old in this way due to egoism has alone brought want, poverty and distress in its wake. This simply means that the part of human arrangements brought about by 'practicians' who calculated on the basis of either their own egotism or that of others must always prove impractical.

Now naturally it is not simply a matter of recognizing a law of this kind, but the real practical part begins with the question: How is one to translate this law into actual fact? Obviously this law says nothing less than this: man's welfare is the greater, in proportion as egoism is less. So for its translation into reality one must have people who can find their way out of egoism. In practice, however, this is quite impossible if the individual's share of weal and woe is measured according to his labour. He who labours for himself *must* gradually fall a victim to egoism. Only one who labours solely for the rest can gradually grow to be a worker without egoism.

But there is one thing needed to begin with. If any man works for another, he must find in this other man the reason for his work; and if anyone is to work for the community, he must perceive and feel the value, the nature and importance, of this community. He can only do this when the community is something quite different from a more or less indefinite summation of individual men. It must be informed by an actual spirit, in which each single one has his part. It must be such that each one says: 'It is as it should be, and I *will* that it be so'. The community must have a spiritual mission, and each individual must have the will to contribute towards the fulfilling of this mission. All the vague abstract ideals of which people usually talk cannot present such a mission. If there be nothing but these, then one individual here or one group there will be working without any clear overview of what use there is in their work, except it being to the advantage of their families, or of those particular interests to which they happen to be attached. In every single member, down to the most solitary, this spirit of the community must be alive...

No one need try to discover a solution of the social question that shall hold good for all time, but simply to find the right form for his social thoughts and actions in the light of the immediate need of the time in which he lives. Indeed there is today no theoretical scheme which could be devised or carried into effect by any one person which in itself could solve the social question. For this he would need to possess the power to force a number of people into the conditions which he had created. But in the present day any such compulsion is out of the question. The possibility must be found of each person doing *of his own free will* that which he is called upon to do according to his strength and abilities. For this reason there can be no possible question of ever trying to work on people theoretically, by merely indoctrinating them with a view as to how economic conditions might best be arranged. A bald economic theory can never act as a force to counteract the powers of egoism. For a while such an economic theory may sweep the masses along with a kind of impetus that *appears* to resemble idealism; but in the long run it helps nobody. Anyone who implants such a theory into a mass of people without giving them some real spiritual substance along with it is sinning against the real meàning of human evolution. The only thing which can help is a spiritual world-conception which of itself, through what it has to offer, can live in the thoughts, in the feelings, in the will — in short, in a man's whole soul. . .

The recognition of these principles means, it is true, the loss of many an illusion for various people whose ambition it is to be popular benefactors. It makes working for the welfare of society a really difficult matter — one of which the results, too, may in certain circumstances comprise only quite tiny part-results. Most of what is given out today by whole parties as panaceas for social life loses its value, and is seen to be a mere bubble and hollow phrase, lacking in due knowledge of human life. No parliament, no democracy, no popular agitation can have any meaning for a person who looks at all deeper, if they violate the law stated above; whereas everything of this kind may work for good if it works on the lines of this law. It is a mischievous delusion to believe that particular persons sent up to some parliament as delegates from the people can do anything for the good of mankind, unless their activity is in conformity with the fundamental social law.

Wherever this law finds outer expression, wherever anyone is at work on its lines — so far as is possible in that position in which he is placed within the community — good results will be attained, though it be but in the single case and in never so small a measure. And it is only a number of individual results attained in this way that will together combine to the healthy collective progress of society.

The healthy social life is found
When in the mirror of each human soul
The whole community is shaped,
And when in the community
Lives the strength of each human soul.

3. CAPITAL AND CREDIT

From various points of view the opinion has been expressed that all questions of money are so complicated as to be well-nigh impossible to grasp in clear and transparent thoughts. A similar view can be maintained regarding many questions of modern social life. But we should consider the consequences that must follow if men allow their social dealings to be guided by indefinite thoughts; for such thoughts do not merely signify a confusion in theoretic knowledge, they are potent forces in life; their vague character lives on in the institutions that arise under their influence, which in turn result in social conditions making life impossible...

If we try to go the root of the social question, we are bound to see that even the most material demands can be grappled with only by proceeding to the thoughts that underlie the co-operation of men and women in a community. For example, people closely connected with the land have indicated how, under the influence of modern economic forces, the buying and selling of land has made land into a commodity, and they are of the opinion that this is harmful to society. Yet opinions such as these do not lead to practical results, for men in other spheres of life do not admit that they are justified... We must take into account how the purely capitalistic tendency affects the valuation of land. Capital creates the laws of its own increase, which in certain spheres no longer accord with an increase on sound lines. This is specially evident in the case of land. Certain conditions may well make it necessary for a district to be fruitful in a particular way — they may be founded on spiritual and cultural peculiarities. But their fulfilment might result in a smaller interest on capital than investment elsewhere. As a consequence of the purely capitalistic tendency the land will then be exploited, not according to these spiritual or cultural points of view, but in such a way that the resulting interest on capital may equal that in other undertakings. And in this way values that may be very necessary to a real civilization are left undeveloped.

It is easy to jump to the conclusion: The capitalistic orientation of economic life has these results, and must therefore be abandoned... But one who recognizes how modern life works through division of labour and of social function will rather have to consider how to exclude from social life the disadvantages which arise as a by-product of this capitalistic tendency... The ideal is to work for a structure of society whereby the criterion of increase in capital will no longer be the only power to which production is subject — it should rather be the symptom, which shows that the economic life, by taking into account all the requirements of man's bodily and spiritual nature, is rightly formed and ordered...

Now it is just in so far as they can be bought and sold for sums of capital in which their specific nature finds no expression, that economic values become commodities. But the commodity nature is only suited to those goods or values which are directly *consumed* by man. For the valuation of these, man has an immediate standard in his bodily and spiritual needs. There is no such standard in the case of land, nor in the case of means of production. The valuation of these depends on many factors, which only become apparent when one takes into account the social structure as a whole...

Where 'supply and demand' are the determining factors, there the egoistic type of value is the only one that can come into reckoning. The 'market' relationship must be superseded by associations regulating the exchange and production of goods by an intelligent observation of human needs. Such associations can replace mere supply and demand by contracts and negotiations between groups of producers and consumers, and between different groups of producers...

Work done in confidence of the return achievements of others constitutes the giving of *credit* in social life. As there was once a transition from barter to the money system, so there has recently been a progressive transformation to a basis of credit. Life makes it necessary today for one man to work with means entrusted to him by another, or by a community, having confidence in his power to achieve a result. But under the capitalistic method the credit system involves a complete loss of the real and satisfying human relationship of a man to the conditions of his life and work. Credit is given when there is prospect of an increase of capital that seems to justify it; and work is always done subject to the view that the confidence or credit received will have to appear justified in the capitalistic sense. And what is the result? Human beings are subjected to the power of dealings in capital which take place in a sphere of finance remote from life. And the moment they become fully conscious of this fact, they feel it to be unworthy of their humanity. . .

A healthy system of giving credit presupposes a social structure which enables economic values to be estimated by their relation to the satisfaction of men's bodily and spiritual needs. Men's economic dealings will take their form from this. Production will be considered from the point of view of needs, no longer by an abstract scale of capital and wages.

Economic life in a threefold society is built up by the co-operation of *associations* arising out of the needs of producers and the interests of consumers. In their mutual dealings, impulses from the spiritual sphere and sphere of rights will play a decisive part. These associations will not be bound to a purely capitalistic standpoint, for one association will be in direct mutual dealings with another, and thus the one-sided interests of one branch of production will be regulated and balanced by those of the other. The responsibility for the giving and taking of credit will thus devolve to the associations. This will not impair the scope and activity of individuals with special faculties; on the contrary, only this method will give individual faculties full scope: the individual is responsible to his association for achieving the best possible results. The association is responsible to other associations for using these individual achievements to good purpose. The individual's desire for gain will no longer be imposing production on the life of the community; production will be regulated by the needs of the community. . .

All kinds of dealings are possible between the new associations and old forms of business — there is no question of the old having to be destroyed and replaced by the new. The new simply takes its place and will have to justify itself and prove its inherent power, while the old will dwindle away. . . The essential thing is that the threefold idea will stimulate a real social intelligence in the men and women of the community. The individual will in a very definite sense be contributing to the achievements of the whole community. . . The individual faculties of men, working in harmony with the human relationships founded in the sphere of rights, and with the production, circulation and consumption that are regulated by the economic associations, will result in the greatest possible efficiency. Increase of capital, and a proper adjustment of work and return for work, will appear as a final consequence. . .

Whether a man rejects this idea or makes it his own will depend on his summoning the will and energy to work his way through into the sphere of causes. If he does so, he will cease considering external institutions alone; his attention will be guided to the human beings who make the institutions. Division of labour separates men; the forces that come from the three spheres of social life, once these are made independent, will draw them together again. . . This inevitable demand of the time is shown in a vivid light by such concrete facts as the continued intensification of the credit system. . . In the long run, credit cannot work healthily unless the giver of credit feels himself responsible for all that is brought about through his giving credit. The receiver of credit, through the associations, must give him grounds to justify his taking this responsibility. For a healthy national economy, it is not merely important that credit should further the spirit of enterprise as such, but that the right methods and institutions should exist to enable the spirit of enterprise to work in a socially useful way.

The social thoughts that start from the threefold idea do not aim to replace free business dealings governed by supply and demand by a system of rations and regulations. Their aim is to realize the true relative values of commodities, with the underlying idea that the product of one man's labour should be equivalent in value to all the other commodities that he needs for his consumption during the time he spends in producing it.

Under the capitalistic system, demand may determine whether someone will undertake the production of a certain commodity. But demand alone can never determine whether it will be possible to produce it at a price corresponding to its value in the sense defined above. This can only be determined through methods and institutions by which society in all its aspects will bring about a sensible valuation of the different commodities. Anyone who doubts that this is worth striving for is lacking in vision. For he does not see that, under the mere rule of supply and demand, human needs whose satisfaction would uplift the civilized life of the community are being starved. And he has no feeling for the

necessity of trying to include the satisfaction of such needs among
the practical incentives of an organized community. The essential aim of the threefold society is to create a just balance between
human needs and the value of the products of human work.

4. ANGELIC IMPULSES IN SOCIAL LIFE

What are the Angels, the spiritual beings nearest to men, doing
in the human astral body in the present age? A certain degree at
least of Imaginative cognition* must have been attained if this question is to be answered. It is then revealed that these beings of the
Hierarchy of the Angels — particularly through their concerted
work, though in a sense each Angel has his task in connection
with every human being — these beings form *pictures* in man's
astral body under the guidance of the Spirits of Form, the
Exusiai . . .

If we watch the Angels carrying out this work of theirs, it is
clear that they have a very definite intention for the future configuration of human social life; their aim is to engender in human
astral bodies such pictures as will bring about definite social conditions in future. People may shy away from the notion that Angels
want to release in them ideals for the future, but it is so all the
same. And indeed in forming these pictures the Angels work on
a definite principle, namely that in future no human being is to
find peace in the enjoyment of happiness if others beside him are
unhappy. An impulse of *brotherhood* in the absolute sense, unifica-
tion of the human race in brotherhood rightly understood — this
is to be the one governing principle of social conditions.

There is a second impulse in the work of the Angels. They
have certain objectives not only in connection with outer social
life, but also with man's life of soul. Through the pictures they
inculcate into the astral body, their aim is that in future every
human being shall see in each one of his fellow-men a hidden *divinity*. Quite clearly, according to their intentions, things are to become
different. Neither in theory nor in practice shall we look only at
a man's physical qualities, regarding him as a more highly developed animal, but we must confront every human being with the
fully developed feeling that in him something from the divine

*See Chapter 2.2 — *Levels of Consciousness.*

foundations of the world is revealed through flesh and blood. With all the earnestness, all the strength and all the insight at our command to conceive man as a picture revealed from the spiritual world — this is the impulse laid by the Angels into the pictures.

Once this is fulfilled, there will be a very definite consequence. The basis of all free religious feeling in future will be the recognition, not merely in theory but in actual practice, that every human being is made in the likeness of the Godhead. There will then be no need for religious coercion; for every meeting between one man and another will from the outset be a religious rite, a sacrament; and nobody will need a special church with institutions on the physical plane to sustain religous life. If the Church understands itself truly, its aim can only be to render itself unnecessary on the physical plane, as the whole of life becomes the expression of the supersensible. The bestowal on man of complete *freedom in religious life* — this at least underlies the impulses of the Angels.

And there is a third objective: to make it possible for men to reach the spirit through thinking, to cross the abyss and through thinking to come to the spirit. Spiritual science for the spirit, freedom of religion for the soul, brotherhood for the body — this resounds like cosmic music through the work wrought by the Angels in the astral bodies of men.

All that is necessary is to raise our consciousness to a different level, and we shall feel ourselves transposed to this wonderful site of the work done by the Angels in the human astral body. We live in the age of the consciousness soul, when men must gradually come to understand consciously this work of the Angels. Where are we to look for it? It is still to be found in man while he sleeps, and also in somnolent waking states... While, in spite of being awake, men sleep through some momentous event, it can be seen how in their astral bodies, quite independently of what they want or do not want to know, this important work of the Angels continues... What really matters is that men shall become conscious of these things. This age of the consciousness soul is heading towards a definite event, and it will depend on men themselves how this event takes effect. Purely through the consciousness soul, purely through their conscious thinking, men must reach the point of actually *perceiving* what the Angels are doing to prepare the future of humanity... But progress towards freedom has already gone so far that it depends upon man himself whether he will sleep through this event or face it in full consciousness. This would entail the study of spiritual science; nothing else is really necessary. The practice of various meditations and attention to the guidance given in the book *Knowledge of the Higher Worlds* will be an additional support, but the essential step has been taken when spiritual science is really conscientiously studied and understood, which can be done without developing clairvoyant faculties — everyone who does not bar his own way with his prejudices can do so. Then their consciousness will become so alert that instead of sleeping through certain events they will be fully aware of them.

These events can be characterized in greater detail. The essential point is that at a definite time — depending on the attitude men themselves adopt it will be earlier or later or at worst not at all — a threefold truth will be revealed to mankind by the Angels.

Firstly, it will be shown how his own genuine interest will enable man to understand the deeper side of human nature. A time will come, and it must not be slept through, when out of the spiritual world men will receive through their Angel a stimulating impulse that will kindle a far deeper interest in each human being than we are inclined to have today. This enhanced interest in our fellow-men will not unfold in a subjective, easy way; but by a jolt a certain secret will be inspired into man from the spiritual side, namely *what the other man really is*. By this I mean something quite concrete, not any kind of theoretical consideration. Men will learn to experience something which can interest them in each human being. That is the one point, which will particularly affect social life.

Secondly, the Angel will reveal to man irrefutably from the spiritual world that the impulse of Christ requires in addition to everything else complete freedom of religion, that only that Christianity which makes this freedom of religion possible is correct. And thirdly, unquestionable insight into the spiritual nature of the world.

This event ought to take place in such a way that the consciousness soul has a certain relationship to it. The Angel is working to this end, through his pictures in man's astral body. But let it be emphasized that this impending event is already put at the dis-

posal of the human will. Many things that should lead to conscious awareness of this event may be, and indeed are being, left
undone.

But as you know, there are other beings working in world
evolution who are interested in deflecting man from his proper
course: the Ahrimanic and Luciferic beings. That belongs to the
divinely-willed evolution of mankind. If man were to follow the
dictates of his own nature, he could hardly fail to perceive what
the Angel is unfolding in his astral body; but the Luciferic beings
aim to tear man away from insight into this work. They set about
this by curbing man's free will. True, they desire to make him good,
for from this aspect Lucifer desires that there be in man goodness
and spirituality, but automatically, without free will. Man is to
be led automatically, in accordance with good principles, to clairvoyance; but the Luciferic beings want to remove from him the
possibility of evil-doing, to make man into a being who indeed
acts out of the spirit, but as a reflection, as an automaton, without free will. . . The Ahrimanic beings too are working to obscure
this revelation. They are not at pains to make man particularly
spiritual, but rather to kill out in him the consciousness of his
own spirituality. They endeavour to instil in him the conviction
that he is nothing but a completely developed animal. . .

What would be the outcome if the Angels were obliged to perform their work without man himself participating, to carry it
out in his etheric and physical bodies during sleep? The outcome
would unquestionably be threefold: firstly, something would be
engendered in the sleeping human bodies — while the ego and
astral body are not within them — and man would not meet it
in freedom, but come upon it on waking. Then however it is
instinct instead of conscious spiritual activity, and is therefore
harmful. Certain instinctive knowledge that will arise connected
with the mystery of birth and conception, with sexual life as a
whole, threatens to become harmful if this happens. . . Certain
instincts connected with sexual life would arise in a pernicious
form, instead of wholesomely in clear waking consciousness. These
instincts would not be mere aberrations, but would pass over into
and configure the social life, would above all prevent men, through
what would then enter their blood as the effect of social life, from
unfolding brotherhood in any form whatever, and would rather

induce them to rebel against it. This would be a matter of instinct... And what will the scientific experts say when such instincts arise? They will say it is a necessity of nature, which must come in human evolution. Light cannot be shed on such matters by natural science, for whether men become Angels or devils it would simply say: the later is the outcome of the earlier. So great and wise is the interpretation of nature in terms of causality! The fact is that such things can only be seen through by spiritual, super-sensible cognition.

The second aspect is that from this work, which involves changes for the Angels themselves, another result follows: instinctive knowledge of certain medicaments, but of a harmful kind. Everything connected with medicine will make a great advance materialistically; but men will acquire instinctive insights into the medicinal properties of certain substances and treatments, and thereby do terrible harm. But the harm will be called useful — a sick man will be called healthy, for it will be perceived that the particular treatment leads to something pleasing, people will actually like things that make man unhealthy. Man will come to know instinctively what kinds of illnesses particular substances and treatments can induce. And it will then be possible for him either to bring about or not to bring about illnesses, entirely as suits his egotistical purposes.

The third result will be that man will come to know definite forces which, by quite easy manipulations, bring into accord certain vibrations which enable him to unleash tremendous mechanical forces. Instinctively he will realize a particular mental guidance of the mechanistic principle, and the whole of technology will sail into desolate waters. But egoism will find these desolate waters of tremendous use and advantage.

This is a fragment of concrete knowledge of evolution, which can be rightly assessed only by those who realize that an unspiritual view of life can never grow clear about these things... Man would so revel in the growth of his instinctive knowledge of certain medicinal processes and substances, and take such satisfaction in obeying certain aberrations of the sexual impulses, that he would extol them as evidence of a particularly high development of super-humanity, of freedom from prejudice, of broad-mindedness! In a certain respect ugliness would be beauty, beauty ugliness. Nothing of this would be perceived, because it would all be regarded as natural necessity. But it would denote a deviation from the path which, in the nature of humanity, is prescribed for man's essential being. . .

Man needs inner loyalty,
Loyalty to leadership by spiritual beings.
He can build on this loyalty
His eternal existence and being,
And thus let eternal light
Flow and work through sense-existence.

5. THE HOLLOW MEN

People have the idea that man is man, that the present-day Englishman or German is man, just as was the Ancient Egyptian. But, in the light of real knowledge, that is actual nonsense, for when the Ancient Egyptian turned inward according to the rules of initiation, he found something there which the man of our time cannot find in himself, because it has vanished. What could still be found in pre-Christian times and in part even in the Grecian soul of the Christian era is lost from the soul-constitution of man. When man turned inward in those ancient times he found his ego; even though dimly and not in fully conscious concepts, still he found his ego. That is no contradiction of the statement that, in a certain sense, the ego was born only through Christianity. As *active* consciousness it *was* born only through Christianity. Nevertheless the man of that time did find his ego; for something of this ego, of the real true ego, remained in him after he was born. You will ask: 'Does the man of today then *not* find his ego?' No, he does not; for the true ego comes to a stop when we are born. What we experience of our ego is only a reflection of it. It is only something that reflects our pre-natal ego in us. . . But this real ego, which could be found at that time, is not today in the man who looks into himself, in as far as his being is united with his body. Only indirectly does he experience something of his ego when he comes into relation with other people, and his karma comes into play.

If we meet another person and something takes place between us connected with our karma, then something of the impulse of the true ego enters into us. But what we call in us our ego is only a reflection; and through the very fact of experiencing this ego as mere reflection in this fifth post-Atlantean epoch, we are prepared to experience the ego in a new form in the sixth epoch. It is characteristic of the age of the consciousness soul that man has his ego only as reflection, so that in entering the age of the Spirit Self he may be able to experience the ego again in a new and different form; only this will be in a way different from that in which he likes to do so in our time. At present man would rather call the reflection his ego than that which will present itself to him as his ego in the sixth epoch. People will in future have more rarely those mystical inclinations that men still have today, to brood inwardly in order to find the true ego — which they even call the divine ego!

Men will have to accustom themselves, however, to seeing the ego *only in the outer world*. The strange condition will arise in which every person who meets us and has some connection with us will have more to do with our ego than anything enclosed within our skin. Man is thus steering toward the social age in future when he will say to himself: 'My self is out there with all those whom I meet: least of all is it in me. While I live as a physical being between birth and death, I receive myself from all sorts of things, but not from what is enclosed in my skin'. This seeming paradox is already being prepared indirectly, in that people are learning to feel how terribly little they themselves really are in this reflection. Anyone can discover the truth by calling to mind his biography factually, and asking himself what he owes since birth to one person or another. In this way he will slowly and gradually resolve himself into influences coming from others, and he will find extraordinarily little in what he usually considers his ego, which is really only its reflection, as has been said.

Speaking somewhat grotesquely, we may say: 'In those times when the Mystery of Golgotha took place, man was hollowed out; he became hollow'. The significant point is that we learn to recognize the mystery of Golgotha as an impulse when we see it in its reciprocal relationship to this hollowing out of men. We must be clear when speaking of reality that the space which could

still be found in man earlier — let us say in the Egypto-Chaldean
kingly mysteries — must be filled up in some way. At that time
it was partly filled by the real ego, which now comes to a stop
at birth, or rather in early childhood, for it is still somewhat in
evidence in the first years of childhood. This space was filled by
the Christ Impulse. There you have the true process. . .

The Christ Impulse is not therefore to be conceived as a mere
teaching, a theory, but must be comprehended according to its
actuality. And only he who understands this descent to occupy
the empty space in the sense of ancient mystery-initiation will
understand the significance of the Mystery of Golgotha in its inner
truth. A man cannot today become a Christ-bearer forthwith, as
he could in the ancient Egyptian kingly initiation; but in any case
he becomes a Christ-bearer when Christ descends into the hollow space within him.

Thus the loss of significance of the principles of the ancient
mysteries reveals the great significance of the Christ mystery, of
which I said in my book *Christianity as Mystical Fact:* What was
formerly experienced in the depths of the mysteries and made a
man a Christopheros has been brought out on the great stage of
world history, and accomplished as an outer fact. That is the reality.
From this you will also see that since these ancient times the principle of initiation itself has had to undergo a change, a transformation; for what the ancient mysteries set before themselves
as something to be sought in man cannot be found there today. . .

6. CONSTITUTION OF AN ANTHROPOSOPHICAL SOCIETY*

1. The aim of the Anthroposophical Society is to be a union of
human beings who desire to further the life of the soul — both
in the individual and in human society — on the basis of a true
knowing of the spiritual world.

2. The nucleus of this Society is formed by the persons — the
individuals as well as the groups who were represented — gathered
at the Goetheanum in Dornach at Christmas, 1923. They are filled with the conviction that there already exists a real science of

*An example of a social organism which leaves its members entirely free.

the spiritual world, elaborated for years past and in important particulars already published. They hold, moreover, that the civilization of today lacks the cultivation of such a science. This is to be the task of the Anthroposophical Society. It will endeavour to fulfil this task by making the anthroposophical spiritual science cultivated at the Goetheanum in Dornach the central point of its activities, with all that results from it within the being of man for brotherhood in human intercourse, for moral and religious, as well as for artistic and spiritual life.

3. The persons assembled in Dornach as a nucleus of the Society recognize and support the view of those responsible at the Goetheanum (represented by the Executive formed at the Foundation Meeting) with respect to the following:

'Anthroposophy, as pursued at the Goetheanum, leads to results which can be of assistance to every human being — without distinction of nation, social standing, or religion — as an incentive for spiritual life. These results can lead to a social life really based on brotherly love. To make them one's own and found one's life upon them depends on no special degree of learning or education, but alone on an unbiased human nature. However, research into them, as well as the competent evaluation of these results, depends on spiritual-scientific training, which can be acquired step by step. These results are, in their own way, as exact as the results of genuine natural science. If they are accorded the same general recognition as the results of natural science, they will bring about an equal progress in all spheres of life, not only in the spiritual but also in the practical domain.'

4. The Anthroposophical Society is in no sense a secret society, but is entirely public. Anyone can become a member without regard to nationality, social standing, religion, scientific or artistic conviction, who considers the existence of such an institution as the Goetheanum in Dornach in its capacity as a School of Spiritual Science to be justified. The Anthroposophical Society is averse to any kind of sectarian tendency. Politics it does not consider to be among its tasks. . .

PHILOSOPHICAL FOUNDATIONS

1. THE ACT OF KNOWING

The naïve man accepts life as it is, and regards things as real just as they present themselves to him in experience. The first step, however, which we take beyond this standpoint can only be this, that we ask how thinking is related to percept. It makes no difference whether or not the percept, in the shape given to me, exists continuously before and after my forming a mental picture; if I want to assert anything whatever about it, I can only do so with the help of thinking. If I assert that the world is my mental picture, I have enunciated the result of an act of thinking, and if my thinking is not applicable to the world, then this result is false. Between a percept and every kind of assertion about it there intervenes thinking.

The reason why we generally overlook thinking in our consideration of things lies in the fact that our attention is concentrated only on the object we are thinking about, but not at the same time on thinking itself. The naïve consciousness, therefore, treats thinking as something which has nothing to do with the things, but stands altogether apart from them, and turns its consideration to the world. The picture which the thinker makes of the phenomena of the world is regarded not as something belonging to the things, but as existing only in the human head. The world is complete in itself without this picture. It is quite finished in all its substances and forces, and of this ready-made world man makes a picture. Whoever thinks thus need only be asked one question. What right have you to declare the world to be complete without thinking? Does not the world produce thinking in the heads of men with the same necessity as it produces the blossom on a plant? Plant a seed in the earth. It puts forth root and stem, it unfolds into leaves and blossoms. Set the plant before yourself. It connects itself in your soul with a definite concept. Why should this concept belong any less to the whole plant than leaf and blossom? You say the leaves and blossom exist quite apart from a perceiving subject, the concept appears only when a human being confronts the plant. Quite so. But leaves and blossoms also appear on the plant only if there is soil in which the seed can be planted, and light and air in which the leaves and blossom can unfold. Just so the concept of the plant arises when a thinking consciousness approaches the plant.

It is quite arbitrary to regard the sum of what we experience of a thing through bare perception as the whole thing, while that which reveals itself through *thoughtful contemplation* is regarded as a mere accretion which has nothing to do with the thing itself. If I am given a rosebud today, the picture that offers itself to my perception is complete only for the moment. If I put the bud into water, I shall tomorrow get a very different picture of my object. If I watch the rosebud without interruption, I shall see today's state change continuously into tomorrow's through an infinite number of intermediate stages. The picture which presents itself to me at any one moment is only a chance cross-section of an object which is in a continual process of development. If I do not put the bud into water, a whole series of states which lay as *possibilities* within the bud will not develop. Similarly I may be prevented tomorrow from observing the blossom further, and thereby have an incomplete picture of it.

It would be a quite unobjective and fortuitous kind of opinion that declared of the purely momentary appearance of a thing: *this* is the thing. Just as little is it legitimate to regard the sum of perceptual characteristics as the thing. It might be quite possible for a spirit to receive the concept at the same time as, and united with, the percept. It would never occur to such a spirit that the concept did not belong to the thing. It would have to ascribe to the concept an existence indivisibly bound up with the thing. . .

It is not due to objects that they are given to us at first without their corresponding concepts, but to our mental organization. Our whole being functions in such a way that from every real thing the elements come to us from two sides, from *perceiving* and from *thinking*.

The way I am organized for apprehending the things has nothing to do with the nature of the things themselves. The gap between perceiving and thinking exists only from the moment that I as spectator confront the things. Which elements do, and which do not, belong to the things cannot depend at all on the manner in which I obtain knowledge of these elements.

Man is a limited being. . . It is owing to our limitation that a thing appears to us as single and separate, when in truth it is not a separate being at all. Nowhere, for example, is the single quality 'red' to be found by itself in isolation. It is surrounded on all sides by other qualities to which it belongs, and without which it could not subsist. For us, however, it is necessary to isolate certain sections from the world and to consider them by themselves. Our eye can grasp only single concepts out of a connected conceptual system. This separating off is a subjective act, which is due to the fact that we are not identical with the world process but are a single being among other beings.

The all-important thing now is to determine how the being that we are ourselves is related to the other entities. This determination must be distinguished from merely becoming conscious of ourselves. For this latter self-awareness we depend on perceiving, just as we do for our awareness of any other thing. The perception of myself reveals to me a number of qualities which I combine into my personality as a whole, just as I combine the qualities yellow, metallic, hard, etc. in the unity 'gold'. The perception of myself does not take me beyond the sphere of what belongs to me. This perceiving of myself must be distinguished from determining myself by means of *thinking*. Just as, by means of thinking, I fit any single external percept into the whole world context, so by means of thinking I integrate into the world-process the percepts I have made of myself. My self-perception confines me within definite limits, but my thinking is not concerned with these limits. In this sense I am a two-sided being. I am enclosed within the sphere which I perceive as that of my personality, but I am also the bearer of an activity which, from a higher sphere, defines my limited existence.

Our thinking is not individual like our sensing and feeling;

it is universal. It receives an individual stamp in each separate human being only because it comes to be related to his individual feelings and sensations. By means of these particular colourings of the universal thinking, individual men differentiate themselves from one another. There is only one single concept of 'triangle'. It is quite immaterial for the content of this concept whether it is grasped in A's consciousness or in B's. It will, however, be grasped by each of the two in his own individual way.

This thought is opposed by a common prejudice which is very hard to overcome. This prejudice prevents one from seeing that the concept of a triangle that my head grasps is the same as the concept that my neighbour's head grasps. The naïve man believes himself to be the creator of his concepts. Hence he believes that each person has his own concepts. It is a fundamental requirement of philosophic thinking that it should overcome this prejudice. The one uniform concept 'triangle' does not become a multiplicity because it is thought by many persons, for the thinking of the many is in itself a unity.

In thinking we have that element given us which welds our separate individuality into one with the cosmos. In so far as we sense and feel (and also perceive), we are single beings; in so far as we think, we are the all-one being that pervades everything. This is the deeper meaning of our two-sided nature: we see coming into being in us a purely absolute force, a force which is universal, but which we learn to know, not as it issues from the centre of the world, but rather at a point in the periphery. Were the former the case, we should understand the whole riddle of the universe the moment we became conscious. But since we stand at a point in the periphery, and find that our own existence is bound by definite limits, we must get to know the region which lies outside our own being with the help of thinking, which projects into us from the universal world existence.

The fact that thinking, in us, reaches out beyond our separate existence and relates itself to the universal world existence, gives rise to the fundamental urge for knowledge in us. Beings without thinking do not have this urge. When they are faced with other things no questions arise for them. These other things remain external to such beings. But in thinking beings the concept rises up when they confront the external thing. It is that part of the thing which we receive, not from without but from within; matching up, uniting the two elements, inner and outer, brings about *knowledge*.

The percept is thus not something finished and self-contained, but only one side of the total reality. The other side is the concept. The act of knowing is the synthesis of percept and concept. Only the percept and concept together constitute the whole thing. . .

2. THE IDEA OF FREEDOM

Among the levels of characterological disposition, we have singled out as the highest the one that works as *pure thinking* or *practical reason*. Among the motives, we have singled out *conceptual intuition* as the highest. On closer consideration it will at once be seen that at this level of morality *driving force* and *motive* coincide; that is, neither a predetermined characterological disposition nor the external authority of an accepted moral principle influences our conduct. The action is therefore neither a sterotyped one which merely follows certain rules, nor is it one which we automatically perform in response to an external impulse, but it is an action determined purely and simply by its own ideal content.

Such an action presupposes the capacity for moral intuitions. Whoever lacks the capacity to experience for himself the particular moral principle for each single situation will never achieve truly individual willing.

Kant's principle of morality — act so that the basis of your action may be valid for all men — is the exact opposite of this. His principle means death to all individual impulses of action. For me, the standard can never be the way all men would act, but rather what, for me, is to be done in each individual case. . .

Men vary in their capacity for intuition. In one, ideas just bubble up; another acquires them with much labour. The situations in which men live and which provide the scenes of their actions are no less varied. The conduct of a man will therefore depend on the manner in which his faculty of intuition works in a given situation. The sum of ideas which are effective in us, the concrete content of our intuitions, constitutes what is individual in each of us, notwithstanding the universality of the world of ideas. In so far as this intuitive content applies to action, it constitutes the moral content of the individual. To let this content express itself in life is both the highest moral driving force and the highest motive a man can have, who sees that in this content all other moral principles are in the long run united. We may call this point of view *ethical individualism*.

The decisive factor of an intuitively determined action in any concrete instance is the discovery of the corresponding purely individual intuition. At this level of morality one can only speak of general concepts of morality (standards, laws) in so far as these result from the generalization of the individual impulses. General standards always presuppose concrete facts from which they can be derived. But the facts have first to be *created* by human action.

If we seek out rules (conceptual principles) underlying the actions of individuals, peoples and epochs, we obtain a system of ethics which is not so much a science of moral laws as a natural history of morality. It is only the laws obtained in this way that are related to human action as the laws of nature are related to a particular phenomenon. These laws, however, are by no means identical with the impulses on which we base our actions. If we want to understand how a man's action arises from his *moral* will, we must first study the relation of this will to the action. Above all, we must keep our eye on those actions in which this relation is the determining factor. If I, or someone else, reflect upon such an action afterwards, we can discover what moral principles come into question with regard to it. While I am performing the action I am influenced by a moral maxim in so far as it can live in me intuitively; it is bound up with my *love* for the objective that I want to realize through my action. I ask no man and no rule 'Shall I perform this action?', but carry it out as soon as I have grasped the idea of it. This alone makes it *my* action. If a man acts only because he accepts certain moral standards, his action is the outcome of the principles which compose his moral code. He merely carries out orders. He is a superior automaton. Inject some stimulus to action into his mind, and at once the clockwork of his moral principles will set itself in motion and run its prescribed course, so as to result in an action which is Christian, or humane, or seemingly unselfish, or calculated to promote the progress of civilization.

Only when I follow my love for my objective is it I myself who act. I act, at this level of morality, not because I acknowledge a Lord over me, or an external authority, or a so-called inner voice; I acknowledge no external principle for my action, because I have found in myself the ground for my action, namely, my love of the action. I do not work out mentally whether my action is good or bad; but I carry it out because I *love* it. My action will be 'good' if my intuition, steeped in love, finds its right place within the intuitively experienceable world continuum; it will be 'bad' if this is not the case. Again, I do not ask myself, 'How would another man act in my position?', but I act as I, this particular individuality, find I have occasion to do. No general usage, no common custom, no maxim applying to all men, no moral standard is my immediate guide, but my love for the deed. I feel no compulsion, neither the compulsion of nature which guides me by my instincts, nor the compulsion of moral commandments, but I want simply to carry out what lies within me.

When in bright circles of spirit
The soul lets rule
The pure force of thinking
It grasps the knowledge of freedom.

When in the full grasp of life
The man consciously free
Fashions his will into being
There exists reality of freedom.

3. THE FALLACY OF KANTIANISM

If we may reduce to a simple formula an immeasurably great and brilliant expression of the critical theory of knowledge, it may be said that the Critical philosopher sees in the facts within the horizon of consciousness mental images, pictures, or tokens; and he holds that a possible relationship to a transcendental external can be found only *within* the thinking consciousness. He holds that consciousness can, of course, not leap beyond itself, cannot get outside itself, in order to plunge into a transcendental entity. Such a conception, in fact, has within it something that seems self-evident: and yet it rests upon a presupposition which one need only see into in order to reject it. It seems almost paradoxical when one brings against the subjective idealism expressed in the conception just cited the charge of a veiled materialism. And yet one cannot do otherwise. Permit me to render clear by a comparison what can be said here. Let a name be impressed in wax with a seal. The name, with everything pertaining to it, has been transferred by the seal into the wax. What cannot pass across from the seal into the wax is the metal of the seal. For the wax, substitute the soul life of the human being, and for the seal substitute the transcendental.* It then becomes obvious at once that one cannot declare it to be impossible for the transcendental to pass over into the mental image, unless one conceives the objective content of the transcendental as not spiritual, since the passing over of a spiritual content could be conceived in analogy with the complete reception of the name into the wax. To serve the requirement of Critical Idealism, the assumption would have to be made that the content of the transcendental is to be conceived in analogy with the metal of the seal. But this cannot be done otherwise than by making the veiled materialistic assumption that the transcendental must be received into the mental image in the form of a materially conceived flowing-across. In the event that the transcendental is spiritual, the thought of the taking up of this by the mental image is entirely possible.

A further displacement as regards the simple facts of consciousness is caused by Critical Idealism through the fact that it leaves out of account the question of the factual relationship existing between the cognitional content and the ego. If one assumes *a priori* that the ego, together with the content of laws of the world reduced to the form of ideas and concepts, is outside the transcendental, it will be simply self-evident that this ego cannot leap beyond itself — that is, that it must always remain outside the transcendental. But this presupposition cannot be sustained in the face of an unbiased observation of the facts of consciousness. For the sake of simplicity, we shall here refer to the content of the cosmic web of law in so far as this can be expressed in mathe-

*The realm which Kant thought to transcend the possibility of being known.

matical concepts and formulae. The inner conformity to law in the relationships of mathematical forms is acquired within consciousness, and is then applied to empirical factual situations. Now, no distinction can be discovered between what exists in consciousness as a mathematical content when, on the one hand, this consciousness relates its own content to an empirical factual situation, and when, on the other, it visualizes this mathematical concept within itself in pure abstract mathematical thinking. But this signifies nothing else than that the ego, with its mathematical representation, is not outside the transcendental mathematical law-conformity of things, but inside this. Therefore, one will arrive at a better conception of the ego from the viewpoint of the theory of knowledge, not by conceiving the ego as inside the bodily organization and receiving impressions 'from without', but by conceiving the ego as being itself within the law-conformity of things, and by viewing the bodily organization as only a sort of mirror which reflects back to the ego, through the organic bodily activity, the living and moving of the ego outside the body in the transcendental. If, as regards mathematical thinking, one has once familiarized oneself with the thought that *the ego is not in the body but outside it*, and that the bodily activity represents only the living mirror from which the life of the ego in the transcendental is reflected, one can then find this thought epistemologically comprehensible as regards everything which appears within the horizon of consciousness.

One could then no longer say that the ego would have to leap beyond itself if it desired to enter the transcendental; but one would have to see that the ordinary empirical content of consciousness is related to that which is truly experienced in the inner life of man's core of being, as the mirrored image is related to the real being of the person who is viewing himself in the mirror.

Through such a manner of conceiving in relation to the theory of knowledge, conflict could be decisively eliminated between natural science, with its inclination toward materialism, and a spiritual research which presupposes the spiritual. For a right of way would be established for natural-scientific research, in that it could investigate the laws of the bodily organization uninfluenced by interference from a spiritual manner of thinking. If one wishes to know according to what laws the reflected image comes into existence, one must give attention to the laws of the mirror. This determines *how* the beholder is reflected; it occurs in different ways according as one has a plane, concave or convex mirror. But the being of the person who is reflected is outside the mirror. One could thus see in the laws to be discovered through natural-scientific research the reasons for the form of the empirical consciousness, and with these laws nothing should be mixed of that which spiritual science has to say about the inner life of man's core of being. Within natural-scientific research one will always rightly oppose the interference of purely spiritual points of view. It is only natural that, in the area of this research, there is more sympathy with explanations which are given in a mechanistic way than with spiritual laws. A conception such as the following *must* be congenial to one who is at home in clear natural-scientific conceptions: 'The fact of consciousness brought about by the stimulation of brain cells does not belong in a class essentially different from that of gravity connected with matter' (Moriz Benedict).

In any case, such an explanation gives with exact methodology that which is conceivable for natural science. It is scientifically tenable, whereas hypotheses of direct control of the organic processes by psychic influences are scientifically untenable. But the idea previously given, fundamental from the point of view of the theory of knowledge, can see in the whole range of what can be established by natural science only arrangements which serve to reflect the real core of man's being. This core of being, however, is not to be located in the interior of the physical organism, but in the transcendental. Spiritual research would then be conceived as the way by which one attains knowledge of the real nature of that which is reflected. Obviously, the common basis of the laws of the physical organism and of those of the supersensible would lie behind the antithesis 'being' and 'mirror'. This however is certainly no disadvantage for the practice of the scientific method of approach from both directions. With the maintenance of the antithesis described, this method would, so to speak, flow in two currents, each reciprocally illuminating and clarifying the other. For it must be maintained that in the physical organization we are not dealing with a reflecting apparatus in the *absolute* sense, independent of the supersensible. The reflecting apparatus must, after all, be considered as the product of the supersensible being who is mirrored in it. The relative reciprocal independence of the one and the other method of approach mentioned above must be supplemented by a third coming to meet them, which enters into the depths of the problem, and which is capable of beholding the synthesis of the sensible and the supersensible. The confluence of the two currents may be conceived as given through a possible further development of the life of the mind up to the Intuitive cognition already described. Only with *this* cognition is that antithesis transcended.

It may thus be asserted that epistemologically unbiased considerations open the way for rightly understood Anthroposophy. For these lead to the conclusion that it is a theoretically understandable possibility that the core of man's being may have an existence free of the physical organization, and that the opinion of ordinary consciousness — that the ego is to be considered a being absolutely within the body — is to be adjudged an *inevitable* illusion of the immediate life of the mind. The ego — with the whole of man's core of being — can be viewed as an entity which experiences its relationship to the objective world within that world itself, and receives its experiences as reflections in the form of mental images from the bodily organization. The separation of man's core of being from the bodily organization must, naturally, not be conceived spatially, but must be viewed as a relative dynamic state of release. An apparent contradiction is then also resolved, which might be discovered between what is here said and what has previously been said regarding the nature of sleep. In the waking state the human core of being is so fitted into the physical organization that it is reflected in this through the dynamic relationship to it; in the state of sleep the reflecting ceases. Since the ordinary consciousness, in the sense of the epistemological considerations here presented, is rendered possible only through the reflection (through the reflected mental images), it ceases, therefore, during the state of sleep. The condition of mind of the spiritual-researcher can be understood as one in which the illusion of the ordinary consciousness is overcome, and which gains a starting-point in the life of the soul from which it actually experiences the human core of being in free release from the bodily organization. All else which is then achieved through exercises is only a deeper delving into the transcendental in which the ego of ordinary consciousness really exists, although it is not aware of itself as within the transcendental.

Spiritual research is thus proved to be epistemologically conceivable. That it is conceivable will be admitted, naturally, only by one who can accept the view that the so-called Critical theory of knowledge will be able to maintain its dogma of the impossibility of leaping over consciousness, only so long as it fails to see through the illusion that the human core of being is enclosed within the bodily organization and receives impressions through the senses. I am aware that I have given only indications in outline in my epistemological exposition. Yet it may be possible to recognize from these indications that they are not isolated notions, but grow out of a developed fundamental epistemological conception.

Riddle on riddle stands in space,
Riddle on riddle courses in time.
Only that spirit finds a solution
That grasps itself
Beyond the limits of space
Beyond the course of time.

NATURAL SCIENCE AND SPIRITUAL SCIENCE

1. MATHEMATICS AND MAN

If we wish to comprehend nature, we must permeate it with concepts and ideas. Why must we do that? Because only thereby do we become conscious human beings. Just as each morning on opening our eyes we gain consciousness in interaction with the outer world, so essentially did consciousness awake within human evolution. . . Something else happens in this process, however. In coming to such concepts as we achieve in contemplating nature, our concepts become clear, but their compass becomes diminished, and if we consider exactly what we have achieved we see that it is an external, mathematical-mechanical lucidity. Within that lucidity, however, we find no concepts that allow us to typify life, or even consciousness, in any way. . . We have achieved clarity, but along the way we have lost man. We move through nature, apply a mathematical-mechanical explanation, apply the theory of evolution, formulate a view of nature — within which man cannot be found. We are confronted with a concept that can be formed only with the clearest but at the same time most dessicated and lifeless thinking: the concept of matter. . .

And now we turn away from matter to consider the inner realm of consciousness. We see how representations pass in review, feelings come and go, impulses of will flash through us. We seem to swim in an element that we cannot bring into sharp contours, that continually fades in and out of focus. . . In the Anglo-American psychology of Association, the attempt was made to impose the clarity attained in observation of nature upon inner sensations and feelings. It is as though one wanted to apply the laws of flight to swimming: one does not come to terms at all with the element within which one has to move. And if one attempts, as Herbart has done, to apply mathematical computation to the human soul, the computations hover in the air, there is no place to gain a foothold. While one loses man in coming to clarity regarding the outer world, one finds man, to be sure, when one delves into consciousness — but there is no hope of achieving clarity. . .

What kind of capacity is it, then, that we acquire when we engage in mathematics? To answer this we must take fully seriously the concept of 'becoming' as it applies to human life. We must begin by acquiring the discipline that modern science can teach us; and then, taking the strict methodology we have learned, transcend it, so that we use the same exacting approach to rise into higher regions. For this reason I believe — and I want this to be expressly stated — that nobody can attain true knowledge of the spirit who has not acquired scientific discipline, who has not learned to investigate and think in the laboratories according to modern scientific method. Those who pursue spiritual science have less cause to undervalue modern science than anyone. . .

We must first of all ask: is that which manifests itself as the ability to perform mathematics present in man throughout his entire existence between birth and death? No, it awakes at a certain point in time. We can observe with great precision how there gradually arise out of the dark recesses of human consciousness the faculties that manifest as the ability to perform mathematics, and something like it we have yet to discuss. If one can observe this emergence in time precisely and soberly, just as scientific research treats the phenomena of the melting or boiling point, one sees that this faculty emerges at approximately that time of life when the child changes teeth.* One must treat such a point in human life with the same attitude with which physics teaches one to treat the melting or boiling point. . . Now we say that the warmth that manifests under certain conditions was latent in that body beforehand, that it was at work within the inner structure of that body. In the same way we must be entirely clear that the capacity to perform mathematics was also at work before-

*See further Chapter 12.1 — *The Education of the Child.*

hand within the human organization. We thus reach an important and valuable insight into the nature of mathematics, taken in the broadest sense. Yes, within the child until approximately its seventh year there works an inner mathematics, not abstract like our external one, but which, if I may use Plato's expression, not only can be inwardly envisaged but is full of active life; something that 'mathematicizes' us through and through...

We do not simply observe mathematics on the one hand and sensory experience on the other, but rather the emergence of mathematics within the developing human being. And now we come to that which truly leads over to spiritual science... There comes to light something of a special spirit in mathematics at the point in Western civilization where the poet Novalis, who underwent a good mathematical training, calls mathematics a wonderful, grand poem. One really must have experienced at some time what it is that leads from an abstract understanding of geometrical forms to a sense of wonder at the harmony that underlies this inner 'mathematicizing'. One really must have had the opportunity to get beyond the cold, sober performance of mathematics, which many people even hate, and have struggled through to stand in awe of the inner harmony and 'melody' of mathematics.

Then there enters into mathematics, which otherwise remains purely intellectual and, metaphorically speaking, interests only the head, something new that engages the entire man. This manifests in the feeling: that which you behold as mathematical harmony, which you weave through all the phenomena of the universe, is actually the same loom that wove you during the first years of growth as a child. This is to feel concretely man's connection with the cosmos. And when one works one's way through to such an experience, which many hold to be mere fantasy because they have not actually attained it themselves, one has some idea what the spiritual scientist experiences by undergoing an inner development which you will find fully depicted in my book *Knowledge of the Higher Worlds*. For then the capacity of soul manifesting as this inner mathematics passes over into something far more comprehensive, which remains just as exact as mathematical thought, yet does not proceed solely from the intellect but from the whole man.

On this path of constant inner work — far more demanding than that performed in the laboratory or any other scientific institution — one comes to know what it is that underlies mathematics, and can be expanded into something far more comprehensive: one comes to know Inspiration. In outer-directed empiricism we have sense impressions that give content to our empty concepts. In Inspiration we have something inwardly spiritual, the activity of which manifests itself already in mathematics, if we know how to grasp mathematics properly — something spiritual which in our early years lives and weaves within us.

> To image as life and spirit
> Matter rigid and dead
> Is the artist's aim.
> To give shape and firmness
> To spirit — flowing, mobile —
> Is the researcher's striving.
> And when the work
> Reaches its peak
> Then must both
> Unite in one.

2. A SCIENCE OF PURE PHENOMENA

In establishing a correlation between our inner life and the outer physical world we can use the concepts we form in such a way that we try not to remain within the natural phenomena but to think on beyond them. We do this if we say more than simply: within the spectrum there appears the colour yellow next to the green, and on the other side the blues. We are doing it if we seek to pierce the veil of the senses, and construct something more behind it with the aid of our concepts, if we say: out of the clear concepts I have achieved I shall construct atoms, molecules, all the movements of matter supposed to exist behind the natural phenomena. Thereby something extraordinary happens. I use my concepts not only to create a conceptual order within the realm of the senses, but also to break through the boundary of sense and construct *behind* it atoms and the like. I cannot bring my lucid thinking to a halt within the realm of the senses, but take my lesson from inert matter, which continues to roll on even when the propulsive force has ceased. I have a certain inertia, and with my concepts I roll on beyond the realm of the senses, to construct there a world — the existence of which I can begin to doubt when I notice that my thinking has only been borne along by inertia. . .

Goethe rebelled against this law of inertia. He did not want to roll onward thus with his thinking, but rather to come strictly to a halt and to apply concepts *within* the realm of the senses. Thus he would say: 'Within the spectrum appear to me yellow, blue, red, indigo, violet. If I permeate these appearances of colour with my concepts while remaining within the phenomena, then the phenomena order themselves of their own accord, and teach me that when anything darker is placed behind the lighter colours or anything light, there appear the colours which lie toward the blue end of the spectrum. And conversely, if I place light behind dark, there appear the colours which lie toward the red end'. Goethe wanted to find simple phenomena within the complex, to adhere to a strict phenomenalism. . .

Despite Goethe's modest confession that he had not acquired a proficiency in handling actual mathematical concepts and theories, he does require one thing: he demands that within the secondary phenomena we seek the archetypal phenomenon. But just what kind of activity is this? He demands that we trace external phenomena back to the archetypal phenomenon in just the same way that the mathematician traces the outward apprehension of complex structures back to the axiom. Goethe's archetypal phenomena are empirical axioms, axioms that can be experienced.

He writes that we must see the archetypal phenomena in such a way that we are able at all times to justify our procedures according to the rigorous requirements of the mathematician. Thus what Goethe seeks is a modified, transformed mathematics, one that suffuses phenomena. He demands this as a scientific activity. He was able, therefore, to suffuse with light the one pole that otherwise remains so dark if we postulate only the concept of matter. We moderns must however approach the other pole, that of consciousness. We must investigate in the same way how *soul* facul ties manifest their activity in man, how they proceed from man's inner nature. This must be a mode of comprehension justifiable in the sense in which Goethe's can be justified to the mathematician — a method such as I tried to employ in a modest way in my book, *The Philosophy of Freedom*.

This book is actually an attempt to win through to pure thinking, in which the ego can live and maintain a firm footing. When pure thinking has been grasped in this way, one can strive for something else. This thinking, left in the power of an ego that now feels itself to be liberated and independent within free spirituality, can then be excluded from the process of perception. Whereas one ordinarily sees a colour and at the same time imbues it with conceptual activity, one can now extract the concepts from the entire process of elaborating percepts, and draw the percept itself directly into one's bodily constitution.

Goethe has already taken the first steps in this direction — read the last chapter of his *Theory of Colours*. In every colour-effect he experiences something that unites profoundly not only with the faculty of perception but with the whole man. He experiences yellow and scarlet as 'attacking', penetrating him through and through, filling him with warmth; while he regards blue and violet as colours that draw one out of oneself, as cold colours. The whole man experiences something; sense-perception, together with its content, passes down into the organism, and the ego with its pure thought content remains, so to speak, hovering above. We take into and fill ourselves with the whole content of the perception, instead of weakening it with concepts as we usually do. . .

Now I said that from birth until the change of teeth a soul-spiritual entity is at work structuring the human being, and that this then emancipates itself to some extent. Later, between the change of teeth and puberty, another such soul-spiritual entity, which dips down into the physical body, awakens the erotic drives and much else. All this occurs unconsciously. If, however, we observe fully consciously this permeation of the physical organism by the soul-spiritual, we see how such processes work, and how man is actually given over to the outer world continually, from birth onward. Nowadays this giving-over of oneself to the world is held to be nothing but abstract perception or abstract cognition. This is not so. We are surrounded by a world of colour, sound, warmth, and all kinds of sense impressions. By experiencing all this consciously we come to see that in the unconscious experience of impressions of colour and sound that we have from childhood onward, there is something spiritual that suffuses our organization. When, for example, we take up the sense of love between the change of teeth and puberty, this is not something originating in the physical body, but rather something that the cosmos gives us through the colours, sounds and streaming warmth that reach us.* Warmth is something other than warmth, light something other than light in the physical sense, sound something other than physical sound.† Through our sense-impressions we are conscious only of external sound and colour. But when we surrender ourselves to nature, we do not encounter the atoms and so on of which modern physics and physiology dream; rather it is spiritual forces that are at work, forces that fashion us between birth and death into what we are as human beings. Once we tread the path of knowledge I have described, we become aware that it is the external world that forms us.

We become best able to observe consciously what lives and embodies itself within us when we acquire above all a clear sense that spirit is at work in the external world. It is through phenomenology, and not through abstract metaphysics, that we attain knowledge of the spirit — by consciously observing what otherwise we do unconsciously, by observing how, through the sense world, spiritual forces enter our being and work formatively upon it . . .

Love for the supersensible
Transforms the ore of science
Into the gold of wisdom.

*See Chapter 12.1 — *The Education of the Child.*
†See further Chapter 10.4 — *Moral Experience of Colour and Tone.*

3. ORGANIC THINKING AS SUPERSENSIBLE PERCEPTION*

Goethe was fully aware of the great advance that he was making in science; he realized that, as he broke through the boundaries between organic and inorganic nature and carried through consistently Spinoza's way of thinking, he was introducing a significant change of direction into science. . .

In a process of inorganic nature — that is to say, a process belonging merely to the sense world — the essential thing is that it is caused and determined by another process belonging likewise only to the sense world. . . I must picture the total process comprising cause and effect in a concept common to both. But this concept is not of a kind that inheres in the process and could determine it. It unites both processes in a common expression; it does not cause and determine. Only the objects of the sense world determine one another. . . The concept appears there only to serve the mind as a means of grasping the whole; it expresses something which is not real in idea, in concept, but which is real to the senses. And what it expresses is a sensible object. Knowledge of inorganic nature rests on the possibility of taking hold of the outer world through the senses and expressing its reciprocal activity through concepts. . .

Now, what is necessary to grasp organic nature? A power of judgement which can impart to a thought something other than merely a substance taken in through the outer senses; one that can grasp not only what appears to the senses, but also the pure idea in itself, separated from the sense world. We may call a concept that is not taken from nature by abstracting, but has a content flowing out of itself and only out of itself, an *intuitive concept*, and the knowledge of it intuitive. What follows is clear: *an organism can only be grasped through an intuitive concept*. That it is granted to man to know in this way Goethe shows by doing it.

In the inorganic realm there holds sway the interworking of the parts of a series of phenomena, the mutual determination of the members by one another. In the organic this is not the case. Here it is not that one member of an entity determines another, but the whole (the idea) determines every single part out of itself

*From the earliest published work, age 22.

according to its own nature. This which determines itself out of itself one can call with Goethe an *entelechy*. The entelechy is thus the force which calls itself into existence out of itself. . . Now the object of the outer world, the entelechy principle which has come into manifestation, is the outer appearance of the organism. But since it is here subject not only to its own formative laws but also to the conditions of the outer world, it is not simply what it should be according to the nature of the self-determining entelechy; but being dependent on other things, it is also influenced so that it appears as if never wholly in accord with itself, never heeding only its own nature.

Here human reason enters and forms in idea an organism not corresponding to the influences of the outer world, but heeding only that principle. Every accidental influence which has nothing to do with the organic *as such* falls away. This idea, corresponding purely with the organic in the organism, is the idea of the archetypal organism, Goethe's *Type*. From this one sees the full justification of this idea of the Type. It is not a mere intellectual concept; it is that which is the fully organic in every organism, without which it would not be an organism. It is thus more real than any single actual organism, because it manifests itself in *every* organism. It also expresses the essential being of an organism more fully, more purely, than any single particular organism. It is acquired in a manner essentially different from the concept of an inorganic process. That is deduced, abstracted out of the reality, it is not active within this; but the idea of the organism is active, effective, in the organism as the entelechy. In the form in which it is grasped by our reason, it is nothing but the essential being of the entelechy itself. It does not summarize what is observed; it *produces* that which is to be observed. Goethe expresses this in the words 'Concept is sum, idea is result of experience; to infer the former requires the intellect; to grasp the latter requires reason'. In this way is explained the form of reality belonging to the Goethean archetypal organism (archetypal plant or animal). This Goethean method is evidently the only one which can penetrate into the nature of the world of organisms.

In the case of the inorganic, it is to be considered essential that the phenomenon in its multiplicity is not identical with the laws which explain it, but merely points to the latter as something external to it. . . The unity, the concept, first appears as such in our intellect. Its task is to combine the multiplicity of the phenomena, to which it is related as sum. We have here to deal with a duality, with the manifold thing we perceive, and the unity which we think. In *organic* nature the parts of the multiplicity of an entity do not stand in such an external relationship to one another. The unity attains reality together with the multiplicity, as identical with it in what is perceived. The relationship between the single members of a whole phenomenon (organism) has become real. Not only in our intellect does it manifest concretely, but in the object itself, in which it produces the multiplicity out of itself. The concept has not merely the role of a sum, a combining element, which has its object *outside* itself; it has become wholly *one* with this. What we perceive is no longer different from that by which we think what is perceived; *we perceive the concept as idea itself.* It is for this reason that Goethe called the capacity through which we grasp organic nature *the perceptive power of thinking.* That which explains — the formal element of knowledge, the concept — and that which is explained — the material, what is perceived — are identical. The idea through which we grasp the organic is thus essentially different from the concept through which we explain the inorganic. . .

Since in inorganic nature any process whatever may cause another, and this in turn still another, the series of events never appears as closed. All is in continual interaction, without a single group of objects being able to cut itself off from the influence of others. The inorganic chain of effects has nowhere beginning nor end; those which follow stand in only accidental connection with what precedes. If a stone falls to the ground, the effect it produces depends upon the chance nature of the object on which it falls.

The situation is different with an organism. Here the unity is the primary thing. The self-generated entelechy comprises a number of sensible structural forms, of which one must be the first and another the last; of which the one can only follow the other in a quite definite way. The unity in idea puts forth from itself a series of perceptible organs in temporal succession and spatial juxtaposition, and separates itself off in a quite definite way from the rest of nature. It puts forth its states of existence out of itself. These are therefore only to be grasped by following the successive conditions of forms proceeding out of an ideal unity; that means, *an organic being can only be understood in its becoming, its evolution.* The inorganic body is shut off, stark, only to be stimulated from without, inwardly immobile. The organism is restlessness within itself, continually transforming itself from within outwards, transmuting, creating metamorphoses. . .

4. THE NATURE OF TECHNOLOGY

Let us start by looking quite superficially at what happens in modern technology. In the first place this is just work carried out in two stages. The first consists of destroying the interrelationships of nature: we blast out quarries and take the stone away, maltreat the forests and take the wood away, and the list could go on — in short, we get our raw materials in the first instance by smashing and breaking down the interrelationships in nature. And the second stage consists of taking what we have extracted from nature and putting it together again as a machine, according to the laws we know as natural laws. These are the two stages, if we look at the matter on the surface.

Looking at it from the inside, the matter is like this: When we take things from nature, mineral nature to begin with, this is linked with a certain feeling of well-being belonging to the elemental spiritual beings that are within it. This, however, does not concern us so much now. What is important here is that we cast out of nature the elemental spirits holding nature together, who belong to the sphere of the regular progressive hierarchies. In all natural existence there are elemental spiritual beings. When we plunder nature we squeeze out the nature spirits into the spheres of the spirit, and thus release these nature spirits, driving them from the sphere allotted them by the Jehovah gods into a realm where they can flit about freely and are no longer bound to their allotted dwelling places. Thus we can call the first stage the casting out of the nature spirits.

The second stage is one where we put together what we have plundered from nature according to our knowledge of natural laws. Now when we construct a machine or complex of machines out of raw material, we put certain spiritual beings into the things we construct. The structure we make is by no means spiritless. We make a habitation for other spiritual beings, but these beings that we conjure into our machines belong to the Ahrimanic hierarchy. This means that by living in this technological milieu of modern times, we create an Ahrimanic setting for everything that goes on in us in a sleeping state, by night or day. So it is no wonder that a person at the first stages of initiation, bringing back into his waking life all that he has experienced outside in the way of noise and confusion, feels its destructive character. For he is bringing back into his organism the results of having been in the company of Ahrimanic spirits. Thus we could say that at the third stage, at the cultural level, we have technology around us, stuffed full of Ahrimanic spirits which we have put there. This is what things look like from inside. . .

Only by penetrating into the depths of his own being will man find the connection with the divine spiritual beings who are beneficial and healing for him. This living connection in spirit, for which we were actually born, is made difficult to the highest degree by the increasing saturation of the world by modern technology. Man is being torn away, as it were, from his spiritual-cosmic connections, and the forces he should be developing within him to maintain his link with the spiritual-soul being of the cosmos are being weakened.

A person who has already taken the first steps in initiation therefore notices how the mechanical things of life penetrate his spiritual-soul nature to such an extent that much of it is deadened and destroyed, making it particularly difficult for him really to develop those inner forces which unite him with the 'rightful' spiritual beings of the hierarchies. When such a person tries to meditate in a train or on board ship, he notices the Ahrimanic world filling him with the kind of thing that opposes his devotion, and the struggle is enormous. You could call it an inner struggle experienced in the etheric body, which wears you out and crushes you. Other people also of course go through this struggle, the only difference is that the student of initiation experiences it consciously.

It would be the worst possible mistake to say that we should resist what technology has brought into modern life, that we should protect ourselves from Ahriman, even cut ourselves off from modern life. In a certain sense this would be spiritual cowardice. The real remedy is to make the forces of the soul strong, so that they can stand up to modern life. A courageous approach is necessitated by world karma, and that is why true spiritual science requires a really hard effort of soul. You so often hear people saying 'These books of spiritual science are difficult; they make you exert yourself in order to develop your soul forces so as really to penetrate into spiritual science'. They want to smooth out difficult passages into something as trivial as can be. However it belongs to the essence of spiritual science that you do not accept spiritual-scientific truths lightly, as it were, for it is not just a matter of taking it in, but of *how* you take it in. You should take it in by dint of effort and soul activity. To make spiritual science your own you must work at it in the sweat of your soul — please forgive me for not being very polite. That belongs to the business of spiritual science.

From Rudolf Steiner's last published communication:

> In the age of natural science, since about the middle of the nineteenth century, the civilized activities of mankind are gradually sliding downward, not only into the lowest regions of nature, but even *beneath* nature. Technical science and industry become sub-nature.

> This makes it urgent for man to find in conscious experience a knowledge of the spirit, wherein he will rise as high above nature as in his sub-natural technical activities he sinks beneath her. He will thus create within him the inner strength *not to go under*.

5. ANTHROPOSOPHICAL MEDICINE

Whatever may arise in course of time from anthroposophy in the sphere of medical knowledge, it will not be in any disagreement whatsoever with that which is understood today as the orthodox scientific study of medicine. It is easy, in looking at the question from the scientific standpoint, to be deceived about this, because it is supposed from the outset that any study not founded upon so-called exact proof must be sectarian, and cannot therefore be taken seriously by the scientific mind. For this reason it is neces-

sary to remark that the point of view which seeks to support medicine on the basis of anthroposophy is most appreciative of and
sympathetic towards all that is best and greatest in modern medical achievements. The whole question turns solely upon the fact
that during the last few centuries our entire world-conception has
assumed a form which is limited by investigation *only* into those
things which can be confirmed by the senses — either by experiment or by direct observation — and which are related to one
another through those powers of human reasoning which rely on
the testimony of the senses alone. . .

But man as he lives in the world between birth and death is
a being who cannot truly be known by means of his physical senses
and reason alone, because he is just as much a spiritual as a physical being. So that when we come to speak of health and illness
we can do no less than ask ourselves: Is it possible to gain a knowledge of health and disease by those methods of research which
concern the physical body alone?. . .

We have four members of the human organization; these, in
order to maintain health, must be in a quite definite relation to
one another. We only get water when we mix hydrogen and oxy-
gen in accordance with their specific gravity. Similarly man can
only exist when there is a normal relationship, if I may use this
expression, between physical body, etheric body, astral body and
the ego. We have not only four but four times four relative states,
all of which can be disturbed. An abnormal relation may arise
between etheric and physical bodies, or between astral and etheric,
or between the ego and one or another of these. All are deeply
connected with one another, and are in a special relation to one
another. The moment this is disturbed, illness arises.

But this relationship, which can be perceived, is not uniform
throughout the human being; it differs for each organ. If we
observe, for instance, a human lung, the physical, etheric, astral
and ego constituents are in different relationships from those of
the brain or the liver. The human organization is thus so complex that spiritual and material are differently related in every
organ. . . Therefore it will be understood that, just as one studies
physical anatomy and physical physiology in accordance with
external symptoms, so — when one admits the existence of spiritual investigation and practises it — one must study with greatest

exactitude the health and disease of every organ. One thus reaches
a complete and comprehensive knowledge of the human organism. This cannot be understood if observed *solely* from the physical standpoint, only through a knowledge of its four principles.
One is only clear about any illness when one can say which of
these four principles either predominates too strongly or is too
recessive. Because one can observe these things in a spiritual manner, one actually places a spiritual diagnosis alongside the material
diagnosis. In the realm of anthroposophical medicine no tools of
ordinary medicine are neglected; of that there can be no question. On the contrary, what is gained by anthroposophical methods
in seeing through the four-fold constitution of man is in *addition*
to all that it is possible to observe of health and disease by ordinary methods.

And further, it is not only possible to observe man spiritually,
but also the whole of nature. One is now for the first time in a
position to find man's relation to the various kingdoms of nature,
and, in medicine, his relation to the healing properties which these
kingdoms contain...

RENEWAL OF THE ARTS

1. THE FUTURE TASK OF ART

This modern age of ours makes a renewal of many things necessary, compared to the past. Through being placed today by world karma in a setting that functions in an especially Ahrimanic way, and through having to make our soul forces strong enough to find our way into spiritual spheres despite all the hindrances that come to us from Ahrimanic culture, our souls need different kinds of support than before. For the same reason, art must also adopt new paths in all its branches.

Art has to speak in a new way to souls today, and our Goetheanum building is meant to be the very first step, really and truly the very first step, towards art of this kind, and not anything perfect. It is an attempt actually to create an art that appeals to the activity of the soul which is connected with the whole conception of modern life, yet a spiritual conception of it. How does what our Goetheanum is intended to be compare with the effect of an older building, or an older work of art in general?

A work of art from the past worked by means of its forms and colours. What was in space and filled out the form was what made the impression, and it is the same with the colours on the walls. Our building is not intended to be like that. It is meant to be — and this is a terribly trivial comparison — like a jelly mould, that does not exist for its own sake but for the sake of the jelly. Its function is to give a form to what is put into it, and when it is empty you can see what it is for. What it does to the jelly is the important thing. And the important thing with our building is what a person who goes inside it experiences in the innermost depths of his soul, when he feels the contours of the forms. Thus the work of art is actually only stimulated by what is there as form. *The work of art is what the soul experiences* when it feels its way along the forms. The work of art is the jelly. What has been built is the jelly mould; and that is why we had to try here to proceed on an entirely new principle.

Likewise, what you will find as paintings in our Goetheanum building will not be there for their direct effect, as used to be the case with art in the past, but to enable the soul, in encountering what is there, to experience what makes its experience into a work of art. This of course involves a metamorphosis — I can only indicate all this — of an old artistic principle into a new one, which we can describe by saying that when the sculptural, the pictorial element is taken a stage further, it is led over into a kind of musical experience. There is also the opposite step, from the musical back into the sculptural-pictorial.

These are things which are not created arbitrarily by the human soul, but have to do with the innermost impulses we have to go through in the age in which we live. It has been, as it were, ordained by the spiritual beings that guide our evolution. . .

2. THE NEW AESTHETICS

By virtue of what does an object become beautiful? This is the basic question in all aesthetics.

We come near to solving this question if we follow Goethe's lead. Merck once described Goethe's creative activity as follows: 'You seek to endow reality with a poetic form; the others however seek to embody the so-called poetic, the imaginative, and this produces only rubbish'. These words convey about the same meaning as Goethe's own words in the second part of Faust: 'Consider what; still more, consider how'. Here is clearly stated with what art is concerned: not the embodiment of the supersensible, but the transformation of the sense-perceptible actuality. Reality is not to be lowered to a means of expression; no, it is to be maintained in its full independence; only it must receive a new form, a form in which it satisfies us. If we remove any individual entity from its surroundings and observe it in this isolated state, much connected with it will appear incomprehensible. We cannot make it harmonize with the concept, the idea we necessarily take as its basis. Its development within reality is not in fact only the consequence of its own conformity to law; surrounding reality had a direct determining influence as well.* Had it been able to develop independently and free from external influence, only then would it have lived out its own idea. The artist must grasp and develop this idea lying at the basis of the object, whose free expression within reality has been hampered. He must find within the reality that point from which an object can be developed in its most perfect form . . . This is what Goethe means when he declares of his own creative activity: 'I do not rest until I find a pregnant point from which much may be developed'. In the artist's work the whole exterior must express the whole inner nature; each product of nature falls short of this, and man's enquiring spirit must first ascertain it. Thus the laws with which the artist goes to work are none other than the eternal laws of nature, but pure, uninfluenced by any hindrances. Artistic creation rests not on what is, but on what could be; not on the actual, but on the possible. . . The content of any work of art is any physical reality — this is the 'what'; in giving it form, the artist strives to excel nature in her own tendency, and to achieve to a still higher degree than she is capable of, the results possible within her laws and means.

The object which the artist sets before us is more perfect than it is in its natural state, but it contains none other than its own inherent perfection. Where the object excels itself, though only on the basis of what is already concealed within it, therein lies beauty. Beauty is therefore nothing unnatural: Goethe can say with good reason, 'Beauty is a manifestation of secret laws which, failing beauty, would have ever remained concealed' or, in another passage, 'He to whom nature begins to reveal her manifest secret yearns for art, her worthiest interpreter'. If it may be said that beauty is untrue, semblance, since it represents something which can never be found within nature in such perfection, so too can it be said in the same sense that beauty is truer than nature, since it represents what nature intends to be but cannot. On this question of reality in art Goethe says — and we may well extend his words to the whole of art — 'The poet's province is presentation. This reaches it highest level when it competes with reality, that

*See Chapter 9.3 — *Organic Thinking as Supersensible Perception.*

is, when the descriptions are so lifelike, through the spirit, that they may stand as actual for all men'. Goethe finds that 'nothing in nature is beautiful which is not also naturally true in its underlying motive'. . . And elsewhere, 'The artist must, to be sure, faithfully and devotedly follow nature in detail. . . only in the higher regions of artistic activity, where a picture becomes an actual image has he free play, and may even proceed to fiction'. Goethe gives as the highest goal of art: 'Through semblance to give the illusion of a higher reality. It were however a false effort to realize the semblance for so long that finally only a common reality were left'.

Let us now ask the reason for the pleasure felt in works of art. We must first be clear that the pleasure which is satisfied in objects of beauty is in no way inferior to the purely intellectual pleasure we feel in the purely spiritual. It always points to a distinct decadence in art when its task is sought in mere amusement and in the satisfaction of lower inclinations. The reason for pleasure in works of art is none other than the reason for joyful exultation which we feel in view of the world of ideas generally, uplifting man out of himself. What is it, then, that gives us such satisfaction in the realm of ideas? Nothing else than the heavenly inner tranquility and perfection which it harbours. No contradiction, no dissonance stirs in the thought world which rises within our inner self, for it is itself an infinite. Inherent in this picture is everything which makes it perfect. This inborn perfection of the world of ideas — this is the reason of our exultation when we stand before it. If beauty is to exult us in like manner, then it must be fashioned after the pattern of the idea. . .

Beauty is not the divine in a cloak of physical reality; no, it is physical reality in a cloak that is divine. The artist does not bring the divine on to the Earth by letting it flow into the world, but by raising the world into the sphere of the divine. Beauty is semblance, because it conjures before our senses a reality which as such appears as an ideal world. Consider what, still more consider how; for on the latter everything turns. The What remains physical, but How it appears is ideal. Where the ideal form best appears in the physical, there art is seen to reach its highest dignity. Goethe says here: 'The dignity of art appears perhaps most eminently in music, because it has no material factor to be discounted. It is all form and content, exalting and ennobling everything it expresses'. A science of aesthetics starting from the definition 'Beauty is a physical reality appearing as though it were idea' does not yet exist.[†] It must be created. It can be called 'the aesthetics of Goethe's world-conception'. And this is the aesthetics of the future. . .

Taken in this sense, the artist appears as the continuator of the cosmic spirit. The former pursues creation where the latter relinquishes it. The closest tie of inner kinship seems to unite him with the cosmic spirit, and art appears as the free continuation of nature's process. Thus the artist raises himself above the life of common reality, and he raises us with him when we devote ourselves to his work. He does not create for the finite world, he expands beyond it. . .

Who, like Goethe, ever grasped art in such deep significance, who ever endowed art with such dignity? It speaks sufficiently for the whole depth of his conceptions when he says: 'The great works of art are brought into existence by men, as are the great works of nature, in accordance with true and natural laws; everything arbitrary, fanciful, falls away; there is necessity, there is God'.

> In primordial times
> The Spirit of Earth-being
> Came to the Spirit of Heaven.
> He uttered a request:
> 'I know how to speak
> With the human mind;
> Yet I beseech of you also
> That cosmic language
> Through which the cosmic heart
> Knows how to speak to human heart.'
> Then the kindly Spirit of Heaven
> Bestowed on the questing Spirit of Earth
> Art.

[†]Written in 1889.

3. ART AS ORGAN OF THE GODS

In the present age man is increasingly compelled to bring about order, stability, peace and harmony by means of external laws, decrees or institutions, definitions in words. This implies no thought of criticism, for it must be so in our age. But something must be added to this — something that signifies the onward evolution of humanity in a different sense. It is probable that our building* will not be able to attain its goal — indeed we are only aiming at a primitive beginning. Yet if human culture is able to take what is expressed in our building (in so far as we fulfil the tasks set us by the higher spirits) and develop it; if the ideas underlying such works of art find followers, then people who allow themselves to be impressed by these works of art and have learnt to understand their language will never do wrong to their fellow men either in heart or intellect, because the forms of art will teach them how to love; they will learn to live in harmony and peace with their fellow beings. Peace and harmony will pour into all hearts through these forms; such buildings will be 'lawgivers', and their forms will be able to achieve what external institutions can never achieve.

However much study may be given to the elimination of crime and wrong-doing from the world, true redemption, the turning of evil into good, will in future depend upon whether true art is able to pour a spiritual fluid into the hearts and souls of men. When men's hearts and souls are surrounded by the achievements of true architecture, sculpture and the like, they will cease to lie if it happens that they are untruthfully inclined; they will cease to disturb the peace of their fellow men if this is their tendency. Edifices and buildings will begin to *speak*, and in a language of which people today have no sort of inkling.

Human beings are wont to gather together today in congresses for the purpose of putting their affairs in order, for they imagine that what passes from mouth to ear can create peace and harmony. But peace and harmony, and man's rightful position can only be established when the Gods speak to us. When will the Gods speak to us?

When does a human being speak to us? When he possesses
*Destroyed by arson on New Year's Eve, 1922.

a larynx. He would never be able to speak to us without a larynx. The spirits of nature have given us the larynx, and we make this gift an organic part of the whole cosmos when we find the true forms of art, for they become instruments through which the Gods speak to us. We must, however, first learn how to make ourselves part of the great cosmos, and then our desire to lead all mankind through these doors will be the stronger. Out of this desire — for its fulfilment is not yet — the longing will develop to work so intensely for our spiritual movement that this aim may gradually be attained. Art is the creation of an organ through which the Gods are able to speak to mankind...

4. MORAL EXPERIENCE OF COLOUR AND TONE

We can see a time coming when we shall be able to enter fully into the sensations and feelings that can arise from the spiritual-scientific world conception, a time when the way to artistic creation will in many respects be different from the past. It will be much more alive, and the medium of artistic creation will be experienced much more intensely; the soul will experience colour and tone far more inwardly, live it through indeed in a moral-spiritual way; and in artists creations we shall meet, as it were, traces of the artists' experiences in the cosmos... There will be a much more intimate union with the outer world, so strong that it will cover not merely the external impressions of colour, tone and form, but also what one can experience *behind* them, what is revealed in them. Men will make important discoveries in this respect, they will actually unite their moral-spiritual nature with that which sense-appearance brings us. An infinite deepening of the soul can be foreseen.

Let us start from a particular detail. Imagine we look at a surface shining all over with the same shade of strong vermilion; assume that we concentrate entirely on experiencing this colour so that we are united with it, we are within it. We shall feel as though we were in the world; the whole of us, our inmost soul, has become colour; and wherever our soul goes we shall be filled with red, living in, with and out of red... We shall not be able to help feeling that this whole red world permeates us with the substance of divine wrath, coming towards us from all sides in response to all the possibilities of evil and sin in us. In this infinite red space we shall be able to feel as though before the judgement of God, and our moral feeling will become such as our souls can have in infinite space. And when the response comes, it can only be described by saying: we learn to pray...

We can then grasp how we can experience a Being that radiates goodness and is full of divine kindness and mercy, a Being that we want to feel in *space*. Then we shall feel the necessity to let this feeling into space of the divine mercy and goodness take on a form which arises out of the colour itself, to let space be pushed aside so that goodness and mercy may shine forth. Just as clouds are driven apart, space is rent asunder and recedes to make way for mercy, and we have the feeling that this must flow in the red. We shall be present with our whole soul as the colour take on form. And we shall feel an echo of how the beings who belong especially to our earth process felt when they had ascended to the stage of Elohim and learnt to fashion the world of forms out of colours. We shall learn to experience something of the creative activity of the Spirits of Form who are the Elohim, and shall grasp how forms can be the effect of colour...

Suppose we do the same with a more orange surface, we shall feel that what comes to meet us has the serious aspect of wrath at most weakly, but wants to impart itself to us and arm us with inner strength... We become stronger and stronger... We then feel the longing to understand the inner nature of things and to unite it with ourselves... With a yellow surface we feel as though transported back to the beginning of our cycle of time; we feel that we are then living in the forces out of which we were created when we entered upon our first earthly incarnation... If we accompany green into the world — which can be done very easily by gazing at a green meadow — we experience an inner increase in strength in what we are in this incarnation. We feel ourselves becoming inwardly healthy, yet at the same time becoming inwardly more egoistic. With a blue surface you would go through the world with the desire to accompany the blue forever, to overcome your egoism, to become macrocosmic, as it were, and to develop devotion. And you would find it a blessing if you could remain like this for your meeting with divine mercy. You would feel blessed by divine mercy if you could go through the world like this.

Thus we learn to recognize the inner nature of colour, and can foresee a time when the experience preparatory to artistic creation will be much more inward and intuitive than it ever was in past ages... Souls must be stimulated again by a power from within, they must be taken hold of by the inner forces of things.

The world of sound will deepen and enliven the life of soul in a very similar way. In future a person will be able to experience what is behind the tone. Men will regard the tone as a window, through which they enter the spiritual world; then it will not depend on vague feeling how one tone is added to another, to form melodies for instance, but by going through the tone the soul will also experience a moral-spiritual quality behind the separate tones... This will come. We shall experience the tone as an opening made by the gods from the spiritual world, and we shall climb through the tone into the spiritual world.

Through the tonic which we experience as absolute and not in reference to previous notes of the scale, we experience danger, we are threatened on entry with being taken captive; the tonic wants to suck us in terribly through the window of the tone and make us completely disappear in the spiritual world... I am simplifying though; we shall have a very differentiated experience which contains an infinite variety of detail. When we climb out through the window of the second, we shall have the impression of powers that take pity on our weakness and say...: 'I will offer you something from the spiritual world, and remind you of something that is there'... We come to a world where, if we listen, various high-pitched tones ring out, wanting to comfort us in our weakness... You have to take the tones with you and, in union with them, live over there in the beyond. If you enter the spiritual world through the third... — remember that you have become sound, you have yourself become a third — you will feel that there are friends over there who approach you, according to the kind of disposition you had in the physical world,... tones that are friends with one another. People who want to become composers will have to enter especially through the third, for that is where the tone-sequences, the tone compositions are, that will stimulate their artistic creativity. You will not always be met by the same tone friends, for this will depend on your mood, feeling and temperament — in fact how you are disposed to life. This results in an infinite variety of possibilities.

Through the fourth... you will find that memories of these tones continually take on a fresh colouring; at one time as bright and cheerful as can be, at other times they descend to the utmost sadness; now they are as bright as day, now they sink down to the silence of the grave. The modulating of the voice, the way the sound ascends and descends; in short, the whole mood of a tonal creation will have its origin along this path from these sound memories. The fifth will produce experiences that are more sub-jective, that work to stimulate and enrich the life of the soul. It is like a magic wand that conjures up the secrets of the sound world yonder, out of unfathomable depths...

These are the kind of experiences mankind must have, par-ticularly through colour and sound, but also through form, in fact altogether through the realm of art, in order to get away from the purely external relationship to things and their functioning, and to penetrate into the inner secrets at the heart of things. Then a tremendously significant consciousness will come to man of his connection with the divine spiritual powers which guide and lead him through the world. And then, above all, he will have inner experiences such as experiencing the forces which guide man from one incarnation to the next.

He must sacrifice his life
And separate existence
Who would behold the spirit's aims
Through senses' revelation,
Daring to pour the spirit's will
Into his own willing.

5. THE NEW ART OF EURYTHMY

The art of eurythmy as we know it today has developed out of first principles which were given in the year 1912. It is still only in its first beginnings, and we are working continuously towards its further development and perfection. However it bears within it infinite possibilities, and it will undoubtedly continue to develop long after our time, until it is able to take its place as a younger art by the side of the older arts.

Arts have never arisen out of human intentions intellectually conceived, nor from the principle of imitating nature in whatever realm, but always when human hearts were found able to receive impulses coming from the spiritual world, and who felt compelled to embody these impulses and to realize them in some way in external substance. In the case of each single art — architecture, sculpture, painting, music and so on — one can trace how certain spiritual impulses entered mankind from higher worlds, how they were received by certain individuals specially fitted to do so, and how what had cast its shadow from higher worlds into human activity in the physical world gave rise to the arts.

It is true that the arts, in the course of their further development, have for the most part then become naturalistic, and have lost their original impulses, a kind of outer imitation taking their place. Such imitation, however, could never be the source of any true art... Originally the arts were permeated with a more vital, a more powerful and enthusiastic spiritual impulse. They had their true reality; their technique was the outcome of man's whole being, not a merely external and formal one but a technique of body, soul and spirit. This fact might well give one courage to develop ever further this art of eurythmy which has been borne on the wings of fate into the anthroposophical movement. For this movement has to reveal to our present age the spiritual impulse which is suited to it... And this spiritual impulse cannot but embody itself in a special form of art into which it flows; this has been given in eurythmy. That will become increasingly evident. Anthroposophy is called upon to bring a greater depth, a wider vision and an enlivening into the other forms of art. But eurythmy could only grow on the basis of anthroposophy, could only receive its impulses through what can come directly from an anthroposophical conception.

The way in which man is able to reveal his inner nature outwardly for his fellow-men is in speech. Through speech he most easily discloses his inmost nature. And so at all times, in a form suited to the particular age, we find alongside those arts which have as their medium the outer element of either time or space, accompanying these, that art which manifests through speech: poetry. This art of speech — I expressly call poetry an *art* of speech, and we shall see later that this is justfied — is more universal within its own form than the other arts. It can be said that the art of poetry in the case of one poet works more plastically and in the case of another more musically; indeed one can say that poetry can also work pictorially, and so on. Speech is in fact a universal means of expression for the human soul. And he who with unprejudiced vision can gaze into the earliest times of human evolution can see that in certain primaeval languages there was actually a deeply artistic element. Such primaeval languages were drawn out of the whole human being far more than is the case with modern languages.

When without prejudice we investigate human evolution, we come upon ancient languages which sounded almost like singing, which man accompanied livingly with movements of his legs and arms. A kind of dancing was thus added to speaking in certain languages when an exalted or ritualistic mode of expression was intended. In primaeval times the accompanying of the word which issued from the larynx by gesture was felt to be absolutely natural. One will only judge rightly what happened there when one makes the effort to realize how that which otherwise appears only as gesture accompanying speech can gain for itself independent life. It will then become apparent that the gestures which are carried out by the arms and hands can, from an artistic point of view, be not merely equally expressive but much more expressive than speech itself. . .

Those who enter deeply into the matter will realize that the breath which we expel from our lungs through our organs of speech and song, what we exhale when we vocalize and give form by means of the lips, teeth and palate, is finally nothing else than gestures in the air: these air-gestures are, however, projected into space in such a way that what they conjure up in space can be heard by the ear. If with true sensible-supersensible vision one succeeds in penetrating into these air gestures, into all that man does when he utters a vowel or consonant, when he forms sentences, uses rhyme, or speaks an iambus or trochee, then the thought arises: alas, the languages of civilization have indeed made terrible concessions to convention. They have become simply a means of expressing scientific knowledge, a means of communicating the things of everyday life. They have lost their primaeval quality of soul.

Now all that can be learned, all that can be perceived by supersensible vision of these air gestures can be carried into the arms and hands, into movements of the whole human being.* There then arises in visible form just the same as that which works in speech. One can use the entire human body in such a way that it really carries out those movements which are otherwise carried out by the organs connected with speech and song. Thus there arises visible speech, visible song — in other words the art of eurythmy.

I seek within me
The working of creative forces,
The life of creative powers.
Earth's gravity is telling me
Through the Word of my feet,
Air's power of form is telling me
Through the singing of my hands,
Heaven's force of light is telling me
Through the thinking of my head
How in man, the world
Speaks, sings and thinks.

*Details may be found in *Eurythmy as Visible Speech*.

THE PATH OF DEVELOPMENT

1. THE CHANGE IN THE PATH

One first reads aright the Bhagavad Gita and other ancient poems when one is conscious that it was actually the soul transposed back into the spiritual world with a heightened feeling of self that uttered all that to which Krishna, or other ancient initiates who had come to such a feeling of self, gave breath. Those old sages rose above the masses of their contemporaries, and rigorously isolated the self from the external world. They separated themselves, however, not by egoistic thoughts but by a changed breathing process, in which the element of soul was submerged into the inner rhythm of the air. . . Man felt how his thoughts passed through the currents of breath like little snakes; he felt his self to be within the weaving cosmic life; and he expressed what could be revealed of this sensation in certain words and sayings. It was noticed that he spoke differently when these experiences were expressed in speech. And this came gradually to be experienced so strongly and intensely that the experience of the breathing process itself fell into the background. It was gradually felt that the words began of their own accord to breathe, to form themselves into rhythmic aphorisms, into recitative. The words, borne on the changed breathing process and lifted out of it, formed themselves as it were into mantric sayings or mantras. And whereas formerly the breathing process and the experience of it were the essential, it now became these sayings themselves. They passed over into tradition, into men's historical consciousness, and subsequently gave birth to the later rhythm and metre of poetry. The basic laws of speech which we can perceive, for instance, in the pentameter and hexameter as used in ancient verse point us back to what had long before been an experience of the breathing process, which had transported man from the world between birth and death into a world of spirit and soul.

It is not right for modern man to strive to find the path into the spiritual world in the same way as in ancient times. We must rise into the spiritual world not indirectly by way of the breath, but on a path of soul, a path more of thoughts themselves. That is why it is right today in meditation and concentration to transform what is otherwise mere logical content into something in the thought itself that is of the nature of music. Meditation today is, to begin with, invariably an experience in thought, a passing over of one thought into another, of one mental picture into another. . .

If we follow such indications as are given in the book *Knowledge of the Higher Worlds,* we shall achieve the exact opposite of what the yogi achieved. Remaining in thought, we do not drive the breath into the nerve-sense process, but begin to bring the nerve-sense process itself directly into an inner swing and rhythm, and to change its quality. Today we try to sever the last connection (unconscious as it otherwise is) between the breathing process and the thinking process. . . All modern exercises in meditation start with this. Thinking is not thereby torn out of rhythm, but only out of an *inner* rhythm, and is then gradually linked to an *outer* rhythm. The yogi passed back into his own rhythm; modern man goes over into the rhythm of the outer world. Read the very first exercises described, which show how to contemplate the germination and growth of a plant. This kind of meditation separates thinking from the breath and lets it be completely absorbed into the growth-forces of the plant itself.

Thinking must pass over into the rhythm pervading the outer world. The moment thought is really freed from the bodily functions, the breath, and unites with the outer rhythms, it submerges not into the sense-perceptions, the perceptible qualities of the object, but into its spirituality. We look at a plant, it is green and its blossom is red — our eyes tell us this, and our intellect thinks it over; this comprises our normal consciousness. But we develop a different consciousness when we emancipate thinking from the breath and unite it with what is outside. Such thinking learns to vibrate with the plant, how it grows, how it blossoms, how in a rose, for instance, it passes from the green to the red. It vibrates out into the spiritual, the basis of all things in outer nature.

That is how modern meditation differs from the Yoga exercises of ancient times — naturally there are many intermediate stages. The yogi sank down into his own breathing process, into himself, and he received this self as a memory; he *remembered* what he had been before he came down to the Earth. We, on the other hand, pass with the soul out of the physical body, and unite ourselves with what lives spiritually in the external rhythms. In this way we *behold* what we were before we descended to the Earth. There you have the difference.

2. THREE STAGES OF SPIRITUAL DEVELOPMENT

It is possible in a certain sense for every human being to raise himself into the spiritual worlds by going through esoteric development. In particular, three forces in our soul may be developed. The first is the power of thought... In ordinary everyday life a man thinks thoughts caused by impressions of the senses or by the intellect, which is connected with the brain. In my book *Knowledge of the Higher Worlds* you will find how a person, through meditation, concentration and contemplation may make this power of thought independent of outer life; may make the power of thought essentially free and independent of all that belongs to the body. That is to say, by means of such development the soul acquires the possibility of thinking, of forming thoughts within itself, without making use of the body, without using the brain as an instrument. The chief characteristic of ordinary everyday thinking, which depends upon the impressions conveyed by the senses, is that each separate act of thinking injures the nervous system, above all it destroys something in the brain. Sleep is necessary so that this process of destruction may be made good. That which we perceive consciously in an ordinary thought is really the process of destruction going on in our nervous system.

We now endeavour to develop meditation and concentration by devoting ourselves, for instance, to a consideration of the sentence: 'Wisdom lives in the light'. This idea can come from no sense-impression, because it is not the case according to the external senses that wisdom lives in the light. By means of meditation we hold the thought back so far that it does not connect itself with the brain... As in meditative thinking we thus do not set up any process of destruction in our nervous system, such meditative thinking never makes us sleepy, however long it may be continued, which our ordinary thinking may easily do. It is true that people often complain that when they devote themselves to meditation they fall asleep at once, but that is because the meditation is not yet perfect. It is quite natural that we should at first when meditating use the kind of thought to which we have always been accustomed; only gradually do we accustom ourselves to leave off the external thinking. Then meditative thinking will no longer make us sleepy, and thus we shall know that we are on the right path.

Only when the inward power of thinking is thus cultivated without making use of the external body shall we have knowledge of the inner life, and learn to recognize our real self, or higher 'I'. The path to *true knowledge of the human self* is to be found in the kind of meditation described above, which leads to the liberation of the inner thought-power. Only by such knowledge does one come to see that this human self is not bound within the limits of the physical body; that on the contrary this self is connected with the phenomena of the world around us. Whilst in ordinary life we see the sun there, and there the moon, there the mountains, hills, plants and animals, we now feel ourselves united with all that we see or hear; we are a part of it; for us there is only one external world, and that is our own body. Whilst in ordinary life the external world is around us, after development of the independent thought-power we are outside the body, one with that which we otherwise see; and our body, which we are otherwise within, is outside ourselves; we look back upon it, it has now become the only world upon which we can gaze from without...

One can then answer positively the question: Why do we wake up in the morning? During sleep our physical body lies in bed, and we are really outside it just as we are during meditative thought. Upon awakening we return to our physical body because we are drawn back to it by hundreds and thousands of forces, as if by a magnet. Of this a person usually knows nothing; but if through meditation he has made himself independent, then he is *consciously* drawn back by the same forces which in the former case draw his soul back unconsciously into his body on waking.

We also learn through such meditation how the human being descends from the higher worlds in which he lived between death and a new birth, and how he unites himself with the forces and substances given by parents, grandparents, etc. We learn, in short, to know the forces that draw human beings back between death and a new birth to a fresh incarnation. As a result of such meditation one may even look back over a great part of the life which was spent in the spiritual world before birth, before conception. . .

But in order to look back on our former incarnations, another sort of meditation is necessary. This can only be effected if one brings *feeling* into the subject for meditation. . . If, for instance, we take the subject: 'Wisdom radiates in the light', and feel ourselves inspired by the radiation of wisdom, feel ourselves uplifted, if we inwardly glow over this subject and can live in and meditate upon it with enthusiastic feelings, then we have before our souls something more than meditation in thought. The power which we then use in the soul as the power of feeling is that which we otherwise employ in speech. Speech comes into being when we thoroughly permeate our thoughts with inner feeling, inner sensation. This is the origin of speech, and Broca's organ in the brain comes into being in this way: the thoughts of the inner life that are permeated with inner feelings become active in the brain, and thus form the organ which is the physical instrument of speech. . .

If now, instead of allowing the soul-force to come forth in speech, we develop meditation from these thoughts thus permeated by feeling, if we continue this meditation further and further, then we gradually gain the power — still without the physical organ, but through initiation — to look back into earlier Earth-lives, and also to investigate the time between Earth-lives. Through such cultivation of the withholding of speech or, as the esotericist says, withholding the Word, we may look back to the primaeval origin of our Earth, to that which the Bible calls the creative act of the Elohim; we may look back to the time when for mankind recurring Earth-lives began. . .

But these two powers of clairvoyance cannot lead us to

experiences connected with former planetary incarnations of our earth. For this the third meditative force is necessary, of which we will now speak briefly. We can further permeate the subject of our meditation with impulses of *will*, in such a way that if we meditate for instance upon 'The wisdom of the world radiates in the light', we may now really feel, without externally willing it, the impulse of our will united with the act; we may feel our own being united with this radiating force of light, and allow this light to shine and to vibrate through the world. We must feel the impulse of our will united with this meditation. We are then holding back a force that would otherwise go into the pulsation of the blood. You may readily observe that the inner life of our 'I' can pass over into the pulsations of the blood, if you recall that we grow pale when we are afraid, and that we blush when we are ashamed. If this same force which influences the blood does not descend into the physical but remains only in the soul, then begins this third meditation, which we can influence through our impulses of will.

He who goes through these three forms of esoteric development feels, when he liberates the power of thought only, as though he had an organ at the root of the nose (these organs are called 'lotus-flowers') through which he can perceive his 'I' or ego, which is widely extended into space.

He who by meditation has cultivated thought permeated with feeling becomes gradually conscious, through this developed force which would otherwise have become speech, of the so-called 16-petalled lotus-flower in the region of the larynx. By means of this he can comprehend that which is connected with temporal things from the beginning of the earth to the end of it. By this means one also learns to recognize in reality the esoteric significance of the Mystery of Golgotha.

Through the soul-force that is held back which in normal everyday life would extend to the blood and its pulsations, an organ develops in the region of the heart, which is described in my book *Occult Science: an Outline*, and by means of which may be understood the evolutions which are called esoterically Ancient Saturn, Sun and Moon, the previous incarnations of our Earth.

You see, my dear friends, it is not stated that esoteric development is obtained from an impossibility, or from what is non-existent, but from that which really exists within the human soul.

Spirit triumphant!
Send flame through the weakness
Of timorous souls.
Burn up the I-lust,
Kindle compassion,
That selflessness,
The life-stream of mankind,
May rule as the well-spring
Of spiritual rebirth.

3. ESSENTIAL PREPARATORY WORK

While the soul dwells in higher regions, harmful forces can nestle into the dense physical and etheric bodies. This is why certain bad characteristics, which prior to higher development had been suppressed by the balancing action of the soul, may now through lack of care become apparent. Men formerly of good moral character may reveal on entering higher worlds all kinds of base inclinations — heightened selfishness, untruthfulness, vindictiveness, rage, and so on. No one should be deterred by this fact from ascending into higher worlds; but care must be taken that such things do not happen. Man's lower nature must be made firm and inaccessible to the dangerous elemental influences. This is done by conscious training in certain virtues specified in the writings which deal with spiritual development; and this is why attention must be paid to them. They are as follows.

First, the person must fully consciously and continually be intent upon distinguishing in all things the imperishable from the transitory, and direct his attention to the former. In all things and beings he can suppose and discern something that remains when the transitory appearance has gone. If I see a plant I can first observe it as it presents itself to the senses; and one should certainly not neglect this, for no one will discover the eternal in things if he has not first made himself thoroughly familiar with the perishable. Those who constantly show concern that one who directs his gaze to the spiritual and imperishable will lose 'the freshness and naturalness of life' do not yet know what is at issue. When I look at a plant in this way it can become evident that there is in it a lasting impulse of life which will reappear in a new plant when the present one has long since crumbled to dust.* We must adopt this attitude to things in our whole cast of mind. Secondly, we must turn our hearts to all that is valuable and genuine, and learn to esteem it more highly than that which is fleeting and insignificant. In all our feelings and actions we should hold before us the value of any one thing in relation to the whole. Thirdly, we should develop six qualities in ourselves: control of the thought world, control of actions, steadfastness, impartiality, trust in the surrounding world, and inner balance.

We gain *control of the thought world* if we take trouble to combat that will-o'-the-wisping of thoughts and feelings which in the ordinary person constantly surges up and down. In everyday life man is not master of his thoughts — he is driven by them. Naturally it cannot be otherwise; for life itself drives man, and as an active person he must yield to this impulse of life. . . . But if a man would rise to a higher world, he must at least set apart short periods in which to master his world of thoughts and feelings. He then in complete inner freedom sets a thought at the centre of his soul, whereas otherwise ideas intrude from without. Then he tries to keep at a distance all the other thoughts and feelings that rise up, and only to combine with the first thought what he admits as relevant. Such an exercise works beneficially on the soul, and through it on the body. It brings the latter into such a harmonious condition that it withdraws from injurious influences, even when the soul is not directly acting upon it.

Control of actions consists in a similar regulation of these in inner freedom. A good beginning is made when we set ourselves to do regularly something which it would not have occurred to us to do in ordinary life. In the latter, man is indeed incited to actions from without. But the smallest action we undertake on our very own initiative does more in the direction indicated than anything instigated through the external pressures of life.

Steadfastness consists in holding oneself at a distance from those moods which may be described as alternating between 'exulting to highest heaven' and 'grieving even unto death'. Man is driven to and fro between all kinds of moods. Pleasure makes him glad, pain depresses him; this has its justification. But he who seeks

*See Chapter 9.3 — *Organic Thinking as Supersensible Perception*.

the path to higher knowledge must be able to restrain himself in joy and grief. He must become stable. He must be able to give himself over in moderation to enjoyable impressions and also to painful experiences, and carry himself with dignity through both. Nothing must overwhelm or disconcert him. This does not justify any lack of feeling, but simply makes him the steady centre amidst the tide of life which ebbs and flows about him. He always has himself in hand.

A quite specially important quality is the *sense of positivity*. He can develop this who in all things turns his attention to their good, beautiful and purposeful characteristics, and not that which is blameworthy, ugly or contradictory. In Persian poetry there is a beautiful legend concerning Christ which illustrates the meaning of this quality. A dead dog lies in the road, and among the passers-by is Christ. All the others turn away from the ugly sight of the animal; only Christ speaks admiringly of its beautiful teeth. It is possible to look at everything in this way, and he who earnestly seeks for it may find in all things, even the most repulsive, something worthy of recognition. What is fruitful in things is not what they lack, but what they have.

It is also important to develop the quality of *impartiality*. Everyone has had his own experiences, and formed from them a definite number of opinions which become his guiding principles in life. And as on the one hand it is self-evident to be guided by experience, it is as important for one who would pass through spiritual development to preserve an open mind for everything new, and unfamiliar that confronts him. He will be as cautious as possible with the judgements 'That is impossible', 'That cannot be'. Whatever opinion he may have formed from previous experiences, he will be ready at any moment, when he encounters something new, to reach a new opinion. All love of one's own opinion must disappear.

When the five qualities already mentioned have been acquired, a sixth appears of itself: *inner balance*, harmony of the spiritual forces. The person must find within himself a spiritual centre of gravity that gives him firmness and security in face of all that would pull him hither and thither in life. He must not shrink from sharing in all the life around him and letting everything affect him. The right course is not to flee from all the distracting facts of life, but on the contrary lies in full devotion to life, and *nevertheless* to guard firmly and securely the inner balance and harmony.

Lastly the seeker must take into consideration the 'will for freedom'. Whoever finds within himself the support and basis for all that he accomplishes has this. It is so hard to achieve, because balance is necessary between opening the senses to everything great and good, and simultaneous rejection of every compulsion. We say so lightly 'influence from without is incompatible with freedom'. The essential thing is that they be reconciled within the soul. When someone tells me something and I accept it on the compulsion of his authority, I am *not free*. But I am no less *un*free if I close myself to the good that I can receive in this way; for then the 'worse' in my own soul exercises compulsion over me. Freedom means not only that I am free from the compulsion of an outside authority, but above all that I am not subservient to my own prejudices, opinions, sensations and feelings. The right way is not through blind subjection to what is received, but to let myself be stimulated by it, receive it impartially, so that I may acknowledge it 'freely'. An outside authority should only lead us to say: 'I make myself free just by following what is good in this, by making it my own'. An authority based on spiritual science will never work otherwise than in this way. It gives whatever it has to give, not in order itself to gain power over the recipient, but solely so that through the gift the recipient may become richer and freer. . .

4. MODERN MEDITATION

Ascent to a supersensible state of consciousness has to start from ordinary waking consciousness. The soul lives in this consciousness before the ascent, and spiritual training provides the means which lead beyond it. In the training under consideration here, among the first means are those which may be characterized as activities of everyday consciousness. The most significant consist in quiet activities of soul. The soul must devote itself to certain definite thought-pictures, of a kind which exercises an awakening power upon certain hidden capacities of the soul. They differ from the thought-pictures of everyday life, whose task is to portray some external object — indeed the more faithfully they do so the truer they are; it belongs to their very nature to be true in this sense.

The thought-pictures to which the soul must devote itself for spiritual training have no such task. These are so formed that they do not depict an external object, but have in themselves the property of awakening the soul. The best for this purpose are *symbolic* pictures; others can however also be used. For the actual content is of little importance; the main point is simply that the soul directs its whole power upon them, and has nothing else whatever in its consciousness. Whilst in everyday life the soul's powers are spread among many things and thought-pictures change quickly, in spiritual training everything depends on the entire concentration of the soul on a single thought-picture, which must be placed by an act of will at the very centre of consciousness. Symbolic thought-pictures are therefore better than those that depict external objects or processes; for the latter have their basis in the outer world, so that the soul has less need to rely upon itself alone than in the case of symbolic thought-pictures, which have been built up by the soul's own exertions. The essential thing is not *what* the picture is, but that it is formed in a way that frees the soul from any dependence on the physical.

We shall succeed in grasping this absorption in a thought-picture if we call up before us the concept of *memory*. Say we have been looking at a tree, and have turned away so that we can no longer see it. We can call up before the mind's eye the thought-picture of the tree from memory. This mental image we have when the tree is not in view is a memory of the tree. Now suppose we hold on to this memory in the soul, we let the soul rest, as it were, in the memory picture, and try to shut out every other thought. Our soul is now *absorbed* in the memory picture of the tree. There you have an example of absorption in a thought-picture, one which reproduces an object perceived by the senses. But if we do the same with a thought-picture we ourselves have placed in consciousness through free will, we shall in time be able to achieve the effect on which everything depends.

An example of meditation on a symbolic thought-picture will now be illustrated. Such a thought-picture must first be built up in the soul, and this we do as follows: We think of a plant, how it roots in the earth, how it sends out one leaf after another, how at length it blossoms. Now imagine a man standing beside the plant. We make alive in our soul the thought that the man has characteristics and capabilities which can be called more perfect than those of the plant. We think how he can move about here or there according to his feelings and will, whereas the plant is rooted to the ground. We may however also say to ourselves: Yes, the man is indeed more perfect than the plant; yet I also find in him qualities I do not find in the plant, the very absence of which in the plant makes it appear more perfect in other respects than the man. For he is filled with desires and passions, which he follows in his conduct. I can speak of his being led astray by his impulses and passions. I see how the plant follows the pure laws of growth from leaf to leaf, how it opens its blossoms dispassionately to the chaste rays of the sun. I can say that whilst man is in some respects more perfect than the plant, he has bought this perfection at the price of letting impulses and desires and passions enter into his nature, in place of what appear to me as the pure forces at work in the plant. I now picture to myself that the green sap flows through the plant, and that this green sap is the expression of the pure, passionless laws of its growth. And I then think how the red blood flows through the veins of the man, and how this is the expression of the impulses and desires and passions. I let all this arise as a living thought in my soul. I then picture further to myself how the man is able to develop; how through his higher soul faculties he can refine and purify his impulses and passions. I reflect how a baser element in these impulses and passions is thus eradicated, and they are reborn at a higher level. The blood can then be thought of as the expression of these purified and chastened impulses and passions. I now look in spirit at, for example, a rose, and say to myself: in the red petal of the rose I see the green colour of the sap changed to red; and the red rose follows, no less than the green leaf, the pure passionless laws of growth. The red rose may now become for me a symbol of a blood that is the expression of the chastened impulses and passions that have thrown off their baser part, and resemble in their purity the forces that are at work in the red rose.

I now try not merely to work such thoughts over in my intellect, but to let them come to life *in my feelings*. I can have a sensation of bliss when I picture the pure and dispassionate nature of the growing plant; I can bring to birth the feeling that certain higher perfections have to be purchased by the acquisition of impulses and desires. This can transform the bliss I previously experienced into a solemn feeling; and then a feeling of liberation can come over me, a feeling of true happiness, when I surrender myself to the thought of the red blood that can become the bearer of experiences that are inwardly pure, like the red sap of the rose. It is important that we do not confront without feelings the thought which serves to build up such a symbolic picture. After we have entered right into such thoughts and feelings, we then recast them into the following symbol:

Imagine before you a black cross. Let this black cross be a *symbol* for the baser elements that have been cast out from the impulses and passions; and at the point where the beams of the cross intersect, picture to yourself seven resplendent red roses arranged in a circle. Let these roses be the *symbol* for you of a blood that expresses the purified and cleansed passions and impulses.* Such a symbolic thought-picture should be called up before the soul in the same way as was explained for a memory-picture. If one surrenders oneself to it in inner absorption, such a thought-picture has the power to awaken the soul. We must try whilst so absorbed to banish every other thought. The symbol in question alone should now hover in spirit before the soul as livingly as possible.

It is not without meaning that the symbol has not simply been put forward as a picture that has an awakening power, but that it was first built up by a sequence of thoughts concerning plant and man. For the effect of such a picture depends on our having first put it together ourself in the way described, before we use it as an object of meditation. Were we to picture it without having gone through this construction of it in our own soul it would

Author's footnote: How far these thoughts are justified from the side of natural science is of no consequence. The whole point is to form thoughts about plant and man which can be arrived at by simple and direct observation, without any theory. Thoughts of this kind also have their significance, alongside of the theoretical ideas of science concerning objects in the world around us, which are in their right place no less significant. Here the thoughts are not there to present facts in scientific terms, but to create a *symbol* that will prove effective in influencing the soul, irrespective of any criticism that could be directed at the composition of this symbol.

remain cold, and would have far less effect than if through the preparation it has received the power to enlighten the soul. During the meditation we should not recall the preparatory steps, but then merely have the symbolic picture hovering before us in spirit, quick with life, and let resonate with it the *feelings* that were aroused by the preparatory thoughts. In this way the symbolic picture comes to be a sign alongside the feeling experience.

The effect of the experience depends upon how long the soul continues in it. The longer it does so without the intermixture of any other disturbing idea, the more effective is the whole process. It is however good if, apart from the times devoted to the actual meditation, we frequently build up the picture again with the thoughts and feelings, so that the feelings do not pale. The more patiently we renew the picture in this way, the greater significance will it have for the soul. (In my book *Knowledge of the Higher Worlds* other examples for meditation are given. Particularly effective are the meditations on the coming-into-being and passing-away of a plant, on the forces of growth that lie dormant in a seed, on the forms of crystals, etc. In the present book the nature of meditation is only illustrated by a single example).

A symbol such as that described does not represent any external object or being that nature has produced; and to this very fact it owes its power to awaken certain purely soul capacities. Some people may disagree, they may say for instance: the symbol as a whole is indeed not to be found in nature, but all its details are borrowed from nature — the black colour, the roses and so forth; these have all been perceived by the senses. Anyone disturbed by such an objection should reflect that it is not the pictures derived from sense-perception that lead to the awakening of higher soul faculties, but the effect is due solely to the *way of combining* the single details, and this does not reflect anything present in the sense world.

The process of effective meditation was here illustrated with the example of a symbolic picture. In spiritual training a great variety of pictures of this kind can be used, and they can be built up in many different ways. Certain sentences, formulae, even single words, may also be given as subjects for meditation. In every case these means of meditation have the aim of wresting the soul free from sense-perception, and rousing it to an activity for which the impressions of the physical senses are without significance; the important thing is to unfold dormant faculties of soul.

Meditations that are directed wholly to certain feelings or emotions are also possible; they prove particularly effective. Take the feeling of joy. In ordinary life the soul rejoices if an outer occasion for joy is present. If a man who has a healthily developed life of feeling observes someone performing an action that is inspired by real goodness of heart, he will be pleased, he will rejoice at such a deed. But he may then go on to ponder over a deed of this nature. A deed that proceeds from kindness of heart, he may say to himself, is one in which the performer does not follow his own interests but the interests of his fellow-man. Such an action may be called morally good. But now the contemplative soul can free itself entirely from the particular action in the outer world that gave such joy or pleasure, and form the comprehensive idea of 'Goodness of heart'. He can think perhaps how goodness of heart arises through one soul absorbing the interests of the other and making them its own. And the soul can now feel joy in this moral idea of goodness of heart. The joy it now has is no longer in this or that event in the sense world, it is joy in an *idea* as such. If we try to let joy of this kind live on in our soul for a considerable time, we shall be practising meditation on a feeling. It is not the mere idea that is then effective in awakening the inner soul faculties, but the prolonged surrender of the soul to a feeling which is not just due to a particular outer impression.

Since supersensible cognition can penetrate more deeply into the real nature of things than ordinary thinking, its experiences can give rise to feelings which work to a much higher degree on the unfolding of soul faculties if they are used for meditation. Necessary as is the latter for the higher stages of training, we should nevertheless be aware that energetic meditation upon simple feelings and emotions such as that concerning goodness of heart can lead very far. Since people differ in nature and character, the means that prove most effective for the individual will naturally vary. As to the length of time that should be given to meditation, it should be borne in mind that the effect is the stronger the more tranquil and level-headed the meditation. But any excess in this direction should be avoided. A certain inner tact resulting from the exercises themselves will teach the student how far he may go in this respect.

We shall as a rule have to carry out such exercises for a long time before we can ourselves notice any result. Patience and perseverance belong unconditionally to spiritual training. Anyone who does not evoke these qualities within himself, going through his exercises so quietly and so regularly that patience and perseverance constitute the fundamental mood of his soul, will not achieve much.

It will be clear from what has been said that deep absorption — meditation — is a means for the attainment of knowledge of higher worlds, but also that not just the content of any thought-picture one likes can be taken for meditation, but only one that has been built up in the way described.

5. VISIONS, PREMONITIONS AND SECOND SIGHT

As a relic from the time when a man entered the spiritual world in a more instinctive, unconscious way, and even in his day-consciousness had more in him of the spiritual world, there still rises up today a certain heritage from the past. This is something we must imperatively understand through conscious spiritual cognition; for if not rightly understood it manifests in many deceptive ways, and in these matters such errors can become very dangerous. . .

Among these phenomena, situated at the frontier between the sense-world and the supersensible, are *visions*. In a state of *hallucination* more or less controlled by the person concerned, pictures arise having quite definite forms which are coloured, even audible, but correspond to nothing external. For normal perception the object is outside, the image in a shadowy way within; and a person is perfectly conscious of how this shadowy mental image is related to the outer world. But the vision arises of itself, claiming to be a reality on its own accout. The person becomes incapable of estimating rightly what reality there is in the pictures which appear before him without his initiative.

Visions come about because the human being still possesses the capacity for carrying over into waking life what he experienced during sleep, and bringing it into a mental image just as he does his sense-perceptions. Whether after perceiving a clock I make an inner picture of it, or whether after experiencing in sleep the form and inner reality of an external object I wake up and make a picture of that experience, the only difference is that I am in control of one of the processes — hence the image of it is more shadowy and flat — whilst the other is outside my control; I carry nothing of the present into my conceptual life, but something experienced when the soul was outside in a past — perhaps long past — sleep, and out of this build up a vision.

In an earlier age, when the relation of people both to the physical world and to the spiritual world was ruled by instinct, such visions were perfectly natural; it is human progress that has made them uncontrolled, illusory, as they are today. We must therefore be quite clear that modern man is lacking something: when he has some experience in the spiritual world during sleep and returns to the physical, he no longer hears the warning of the Guardian of the Threshold: 'All that you have experienced in the spiritual world you should note well, and carry back to the physical'.* If he carries it back, he knows what is contained in the vision. But if the vision appears to him only in the physical world, without his realizing that he has brought it back, so that he fails to understand what it really is, then he is without guidance and at the mercy of illusion. So we can say: visions come about because a man carries over his sleep experience unawares into waking life, and then forms mental images of it, which are much richer in content than the ordinary shadowy ones, and builds these up into visions complete with colour and sound.

Another possibility is that a man carries over into his life of sleep the manner of feeling and perception he has in physical life, and is warned there not to cause any mischief. If the sleep is very light — a condition far more common in ordinary life than is realized, for we are often just a little asleep when walking about quite normally, and we ought to be more aware of this — we may without noticing it carry over the Threshold our everyday sensing. Then arise those obscure feelings, as if one were inwardly aware of something happening in the future, either to oneself or to someone else, and we have a *premonition*. Whereas a vision comes about when sleep-experience is carried down into waking life and the Threshold is crossed unconsciously, premonition thus comes

*See Chapter 4.3 — *The Guardian of the Threshold.*

about when we are in a light sleep without realizing it, and thinking we are awake carry over the Threshold, again ignoring the Guardian, our daytime experience. This however lies so deep below consciousness that it is not noticed.

But a man may also halt on the Threshold and not notice the Guardian... When he stands at the Threshold in such a way that he perceives what is in the physical world while already perceiving what is in the supersensible, he experiences something which is widespread in certain places, namely *second sight*, a half-conscious experience at the Threshold. Hence these legacies from the past in dimmed consciousness appear on this side of the Threshold as visions, beyond the Threshold as premonitions, and actually on the Threshold as second sight.

IN DAILY LIFE

1. THE EDUCATION OF THE CHILD

At birth the body is exposed to the outer environment, whilst previously it was surrounded by the sheath of the mother. What the forces and fluids of the maternal sheath have done for it must from now on be done by the forces and elements of the outer physical world. Before the change of teeth in the seventh year the physical organs must be brought into definite shapes and proportions. Growth also takes place later, but this is based on the forms developed in this first period — we can never repair later what we have as educators neglected in the first seven years.

There are two magic words which indicate how the child relates to his environment: Imitation and Example. What goes on in his physical environment, this the child imitates, and in the process of imitation his physical organs are cast into the forms which then become permanent. Everything that can be perceived by his senses can work upon his spiritual powers. This includes all the moral or immoral actions, all the wise or foolish actions, that the child can see. It is not moral talk or reasoned admonitions that influence the child in this sense, but what grown-up people do visibly before his eyes. The effect of admonitions is to mould the forms not of the physical but of the etheric body; the latter is surrounded until the seventh year by a protecting etheric envelope, just as the physical body is surrounded before birth by the envelope of the mother. All that has to develop in the etheric body — ideas, habits, memory and so forth — must develop before the seventh year 'of its own accord', just as eyes and ears develop within the mother's body without the influence of external light...

An example will best illustrate the point. You can make a doll for a child by folding an old napkin, and if the child has this before him he has to fill in from his own imagination all that is needed to make it look like a man. This work of the imagination moulds and forms the brain; the brain unfolds, as the muscles of the hand unfold when they do the work for which they are fitted. Give the child a so-called 'pretty doll', and the brain has nothing more to do; instead of unfolding, it becomes stunted and dried up. If people could look into the brain as can the spiritual investigator, and see how it builds its forms, they would assuredly give their children only such toys as are fitted to stimulate and vivify its formative activity. Toys with dead mathematical forms alone have a desolating and killing effect on the formative forces of the child...

Another example may be given. A fidgety, excitable child should be treated differently from one who is quiet and lethargic. Everything comes into consideration from the colour of the room and various objects around the child to the colour of his clothes. One will often do the wrong thing if one does not take guidance from spiritual knowledge, for the materialistic idea will often hit on the exact opposite of what is right. An excitable child should be surrounded by and dressed in the red and reddish-yellow colours, whereas for a lethargic child one should have the blue or bluish-green shades. For the important thing is the complementary colour which is created within the child...

One thing must be thoroughly recognized for this age, namely that the physical body creates the measure for what is good for it by the proper development of desires. We should pay the closest attention to what the healthy craving, desire and delight want to have. Pleasure and delight most rightly call forth the physical forms of the organs. It is all too easy to do harm, especially in regard to instincts for food. The child may be overfed with things that make him lose completely his healthy instinct for food, whereas through right nourishment this can be so preserved that he always wants, even to a glass of water, what is wholesome for him in the circumstances, and turns from what can do him harm...

The child needs teachers with a happy look and above all an honest unaffected love. A love which as it were streams through the physical environment with warmth may truly be said to 'hatch out' the forms of the physical organs... It is by hearing that the child best learns to speak; no rules or artificial instruction of any kind can be of any good effect. For early childhood it is specially important that for example children's songs should make as beautiful and rhythmical an impression on the senses as possible; the beauty of the sound is to be valued more than the meaning. The more refreshingly a thing works on eye or ear, the better. One should not undervalue what a power dancing movements in musical rhythm have in building up the organs.

With the change of teeth the *etheric* body lays aside its outer envelope, and can be worked upon from without. The formation and growth of the etheric body means the moulding and development of the inclinations and habits, of the conscience, the character, the memory and temperament. The etheric body is worked upon through *pictures*, by carefully guiding the imagination of the child... The etheric body unfolds its force if the well-ordered imagination can take as its guiding principle the inner meaning it discovers for itself in pictures and allegories — whether met in real life or communicated to the mind. It is not abstact concepts that work in the right way, but rather what is seen and perceived with the eye of the mind...

For this second period the magic words are Emulation and Authority. What the child sees directly in his education, with inner perception, must become for him an authority that he accepts naturally without question. Natural, unenforced authority must present the direct spiritual point of view through which the young person forms his conscience, habits and inclinations, and brings his temperament into an ordered path. Veneration and reverence are forces whereby the etheric body grows in the right way. Where reverence is lacking, the living forces of the etheric body are stunted...

Bad habits may be completely overcome by drawing attention to appropriate instances that shock or repel the child. Reprimands give at best but little help regarding habits and inclinations. But if we show the living picture of a man who has given way to a similar bad habit, and let the child see where it actually leads, this will work upon the young imagination and go a long way towards the uprooting of the habit... This certainly needs to be done with great tact so that the effect may not turn out the very opposite of what was intended. In telling stories everything depends upon the art of telling. Narration by word of mouth cannot, therefore, simply be replaced by reading.

It is of vast importance for the child that he should receive the secrets of nature in parable, before they are brought before his soul in the form of 'natural laws' and the like. Suppose we want to tell a child of the immortality of the soul, the coming forth of the soul from the body. The way to do this is to use a comparison, for example: as the butterfly soars up from the chrysalis, so after death does the soul of man from the house of the body. No man will rightly grasp the fact in intellectual concepts, who has not first received it in such a picture. By such a parable we speak not merely to the intellect but to the feeling of the child, to all his soul... For real effectiveness it is essential to believe in one's parables as absolute realties. And this can only be, when one's thought is alive with spiritual knowledge... The spiritual knowledge has for all the secrets of the world appropriate parables, pictures taken from the very being of things, pictures not first made by man but laid by the forces of the world within the things themselves in the very act of their creation.

A force of soul on which particular value must be set during this period is that of memory. The development of memory is bound up with the moulding of the etheric body which is becoming liberated between the change of teeth and puberty. If what is due at this time is neglected, a man's memory will ever after have less value than it might otherwise have had — it is not possible later to make up for what has been left undone...

The older boy and girl must learn for the cultivation of the memory much that they are not to master with their intellectual understanding until later years. Those things are afterwards best grasped in concepts which have first been learned simply from memory in this period of life. Talk against 'unintelligent learning by heart' is simply materialistic prejudice... Up to the time of puberty the child should be laying up in his memory the treasures of thought on which mankind has pondered...

Another result of a materialistic way of thought is seen in lessons that rest too exclusively on sense-perception. All perception must be spiritualized. We ought not to be satisfied, for instance, with presenting a plant, a seed, a flower merely as it can be perceived with the senses. Everything should become a parable of the spiritual. A grain of corn is not only what meets the eye, a whole new plant is hidden invisibly within it. That such a seed is more than what the senses see, this the child must grasp in a living way with his feelings, his imagination, and his mind. He must, in feeling, divine the secrets of existence...

With the age of puberty the *astral* body is first born, its development is open to the outside world. Only now, therefore, can we approach the child with all that opens up the world of abstract ideas, the faculty of judgement and independent thought... Nothing more harmful can be done to a child than to awaken too early his independent judgement. Man is not in a position to judge until he has collected in his inner life material for judgement and comparison. If he forms his own conclusions before doing so, his conclusions will lack foundation. Educational mistakes of this kind are the cause of all narrow one-sidedness in life, all barren creeds that take their stand on a few scraps of knowledge, and are ready on this basis to condemn ideas experienced and proved by man, often through long ages...

Spoken by the mother for the child:

May light flow into thee, that can take hold of thee.
I follow its rays with the warmth of my love.
I think with the best glad thoughts of my thinking on the
    leaping of thy heart.
They are to strengthen thee, they are to bear thee up, they are
    to keep thee pure.
I would fain gather my glad thoughts into thy steps on the
    path of life,
So they link themselves to thine own will of life,
That this may find itself with strength in all the world ever
    more through its own self.

2. NUTRITION*

The relation of man to his food is only properly understood when his relation to the other kingdoms of nature, and above all to the

*Heavily abridged; omissions not indicated.

plant kingdom, is borne in mind. The plant kingdom, as a kingdom of life, carries the inorganic, lifeless substances to a certain stage of organization. Now man is so organized physically that he can take up this process where the plant left it and carry it on further from this point, so that the human organization comes into being when man organizes further what the plant has already brought to a certain stage.

In an *animal* we have a living being which also carries on the process of organization further than the plant. Now suppose that a man eats the animal; it is not now necessary for him to exercise the inner forces he would have had to exercise if he had eaten a plant; for the animal has already carried its organization to a higher stage, and man need only begin at this point. Thus he lets the animal do part of the work that he would have had to do. Now the well-being of an organism does not consist in its doing as little as possible, but in its really bringing all its forces into activity. Thus when he eats animal flesh he fetters within him forces which he would call upon if he ate plant food. Through their condemnation to inactivity the organizations in question remain fallow, they are crippled and become hardened. This he carries with him through life as a foreign body. In normal life he does not feel this; but when his organism becomes more inwardly mobile, as happens in anthroposophical life, his physical body begins to feel uncomfortable, because it has a foreign body in it. We are not promulgating any special cause, but are only concerned with presenting the truth. It is best when spiritual science leads a man to have a sort of disgust and loathing for animal food; and it is not of much use if a man gives up animal food for any other reason.

As another example I might mention *alcohol*, which is quite a special thing in the kingdoms of nature. That which other plants save up solely for the young germ — that is, all the productive force — is in the case of the grape poured in a certain way into the flesh of the fruit as well; so that through what is known as fermentation something is produced which has actually within the plant a power only comparable esoterically to the power which the ego of man has over the blood. What is always developed in the production of alcohol is the same thing, in another kingdom of nature, as that which a man must produce when he works upon his blood from his ego. The consequence is that through alcohol we take into our organism something which from another direction works just as the ego works on the blood. This means that with alcohol we take into ourselves an opposition ego, which is a direct opponent of the deeds of our spiritual ego. Thus we kindle an inner war, and in truth we condemn to powerlessness all that proceeds from the ego when we take alcohol, which is its opponent. That is the occult fact.

In esoteric development we feel the weight of the Earth in animal food more than we usually do, and above all we experience the fact that it inflames the instinctive life of the will, which flows more in emotions and passions. We shall see that all a man loses in the way of instincts, aggressive passions and feelings through refraining from animal food is compensated for from within the soul.

If you were to investigate the cosmos as an esotericist, you would find *milk*-substance on our Earth, but on no other planet in our solar system. You would have to say that the living beings on each planet have their own special milk. The inner being of the *plants* on the Earth is not merely earthly, but is related to that of the other planets, there is in our plants something that can also be found on other planets of our system. The *animal* kingdom is radically different from any corresponding kingdom to be found on other planets.

Milk food connects man with the human race on the Earth as a member belonging to a common family. Milk prepares man to be an earthly human creature, it unites him with earthly conditions, but it does not really chain him to the Earth. It makes him a citizen of the Earth, but does not hinder him from being a citizen of the whole solar system. Animal food, which is taken from the kingdom that is specifically earthly, chains man specially to the Earth. To the extent that a man fills his own organism with the effects of animal food, he deprives himself of the power to become free from the Earth at all. Plant diet is of such a nature as to bring into action those forces which bring man to a certain cosmic union with the whole of the planetary system. That which a human being has to accomplish when he continues the assimilation of plant nourishment is to call forth forces contained in the whole solar system, so that in his physical sheath he becomes a partaker of these solar forces. The lightness in his organism which he obtains through a plant diet gradually develops a certain inner perception of taste in the organism, so that it is as though the latter really shared with the plant in a way the enjoyment of the sunlight, which accomplishes so much in the plant.

You will gather that in the case of esoteric development it is important not to chain oneself to the Earth through the enjoyment of an animal diet, if it can be dispensed with; the actual decision, of course, can only be made according to the personal conditions of the individual. On the other hand, serious consequences might ensue if a person were to become such a fanatical vegetarian that he avoided milk and all milk products. A person may very easily acquire a love of striving to get away from the Earth, and lose the threads uniting him to his tasks upon the Earth. In order that we may not become too eccentric it is well for us to load ourselves in a certain way, like travellers upon the Earth, by the use of milk and milk products.

If we consider the animal *protein* contained, let us say, in hens' eggs, we must understand that such protein is in its structure the result of cosmic forces. These forces work first upon the Earth, and the Earth reacts upon the construction of animal protein with the forces it receives from the cosmos. The smallest cell in a hen's egg is built up of the forces which the Earth first obtains from the cosmos. Animal fat is formed according to entirely different laws.

When the soul undergoes development, it experiences all the *sugar* it takes in or already has within it as something giving it inner firmness, supporting it inwardly, permeating it to a certain extent with a natural sense of selfhood. In this respect a sort of eulogy might even be pronounced on sugar. Through eating sugar a sort of blameless egohood is produced which can form a counterpoise to the necessary selflessness in the spiritual realm of morals. Otherwise there might all too easily be the temptation not only to become selfless, but also dreamy and fantastic, to lose the healthy capacity for judging earthly conditions. An addition of sugar to the food gives the power to stand firmly on the Earth with both feet, and to cultivate a healthy estimate of earthly things.

Coffee so works as to cause the human organism to lift its etheric body out of the physical body, but in such a manner as to feel the latter as a solid foundation for the former. As logical, consecutive thinking depends very much on the structure and form of the physical body, so through the peculiar action of coffee the arrangements of facts in logical sequence, logical accuracy is promoted by physical means. Even though there may be healthy doubts about drinking too much coffee, yet for those who wish to ascend to the higher regions of spiritual life it may be good, occasionally, to obtain logical accuracy by means of coffee. If a student's thoughts have a tendency to stray in the wrong direction, we need not take it amiss if he makes himself somewhat more stable by drinking coffee.

When *tea* is taken, thought becomes volatile, less fitted to keep to the facts; indeed, fancy is stimulated by it, very often in a way neither sympathetic to nor in conformity with truth or with sound proportion. In gatherings where flashes of thought and the development of sparkling mentality are in question, tea might be preferred; on the other hand dreamy fancy and a certain careless, nonchalant nature that likes to overlook the demands of sound external life are awakened by tea-drinking. For a soul undergoing development we feel tea less suitable than coffee, since it leads more easily to shallowness.

Chocolate promotes prosaic thought, it can be felt as the true drink of the commonplace merrymaker. We can understand very well that at family festivals, birthdays, christenings, on certain festive occasions, chocolate is the beverage.

Table Grace

The plant seeds are quickened
  in the night of the Earth,
The green herbs are sprouting
  through the might of the air,
And all fruits grow ripe
  through the power of the sun.
So quickens the soul in the shrine of the heart,
So blooms spirit-power in the light of the world,
So ripens man's strength in the glory of God.

3. A MICHAELMAS FESTIVAL

The Easter festival is that in which man contemplates death and the immortality which follows, through the Mystery of Golgotha. We look at this springtime festival aright when we say: Christ has strengthened man's immortality through His own victory over death... But man must understand the Resurrection in connection with the Mystery of Golgotha while he is still alive on Earth; and if he can do this in his feelings, this will also enable him to pass through death in the right way. This means that death and resurrection, contained in the Mystery of Golgotha, should teach man to invert the relationship; to experience resurrection inwardly within the soul during life, so that after having experienced this inner resurrection in his soul, he may go through death rightly. This is the exact opposite of the Easter experience: at Easter we should submerge ourselves in Christ's Death and Resurrection. But as human beings we must be able to submerge in what is given to us as the resurrection of the *soul*.

Just as in spring we acquire the real Easter feeling in seeing how the plants spring up and bud, how nature reawakens to life and overcomes winter's death, so we can acquire another feeling when we have lived through the summer in the right spirit and know that the soul has ascended into cosmic spaces; that we are approaching autumn, that the leaves are turning yellow and brown and withering away, that nature is dying. We understand this dying nature when we look into the fading process when the snow begins to cover the earth, and say: the soul of the earth is withdrawing again into the earth, and will be fully within the earth when the winter solstice has come. Just as we can experience the Death and Resurrection of the God in the Easter season in spring, so can we experience in autumn the death and resurrection of the human soul.

Moreover we must understand what it means for us and for our age that the soul of the Earth is exhaled at midsummer into the world's far spaces, is there united with the stars, and then returns. He who fathoms the secrets of the earth's circuit during the course of the year will know that the Michael force, which did not descend in former centuries, is now descending again through the nature forces.* We can face the leafless autumn inasmuch as we look towards the approach of the Michael force out of the clouds. Calendars show the name of 'Michael', and Michaelmas is a country festival; yet we shall not experience the present spiritually, linking events on Earth with nature's events, until we understand again the year's course and establish festivals of the year as was done in the past by the ancients. Out of such understanding they founded the Christmas, Easter and Midsummer (St John) festivals. At Christmas we give each other presents and other things, but people receive very little today from such festivals, everything has taken on a traditional, external form.

When however the festivals we celebrate without understanding are again understood, we shall have the strength to establish out of a spiritual understanding of the year's course a festival which only now for present-day humanity has real significance: the Michael festival. It will be in the last days of September, when autumn approaches, the leaves wither, and nature faces death — just as it faces a new budding life at Easter — and when we experience in nature's fading life how the soul of the Earth is then united with the Earth, and brings with it Michael out of the clouds. When we acquire the strength to establish such a festival of the spirit — a festival that brings with it once more a feeling of fellowship into our social life — we shall have founded something in our midst which has the spirit as its source. Far more important than other reflections on social conditions — which can lead to no results in our present chaotic conditions, unless they contain the spirit — would be that a number of open-minded people should come together to institute again on Earth something proceeding out of the universe, as for instance a Michael festival. If people could determine upon something, the motive to which can be found only in the spiritual world, something which can kindle feelings of fellowship among those who come to it — arising out of the fullness and freshness of the human heart through immediate contact — then something would exist which could bind men together again socially. . . But courage would have to be found amongst them not merely to discuss external social reforms and so on, but to do something that connects the earth

*See Chapter 6.1 — *Michael and the New Christ-Consciousness.*

with the heavens, that reconnects physical with spiritual conditions . . .

If today one could see the working of the whole universe when autumn approaches, if one could decipher the whole face of the universe and acquire creative force out of it, then the establishment of such a festival would reveal not only the will of human beings, but also the will of gods and spirits. Then the spirit would again be among mankind!

We men of present time
Need rightly to hear
The dawn-call of the spirit,
The call of Michael.
Spirit-knowing seeks
To open the soul to hear truly
This morning-call.

EPILOGUE

MAN, TEMPLE OF THE GODS

We never in fact bring our real and inmost ego with us from the spiritual world into the physical and earthly; we leave it in the spiritual world. Before we came down into earthly life it was in the spiritual world, and it is there again between our falling asleep and awakening. It stays there always. If by day, at the present stage of consciousness, we call ourselves an 'I', this word is but an indication of something which is not here in the physical world; it only has its *picture* in this world...

This will be clearer if we imagine ourselves asleep. The ego is away from the physical and etheric body, the astral body too. Now the ego works in the blood of man and in his movements. In sleep our movements cease; the blood however goes on working, yet the ego is not there. What happens to it while we are asleep? Something must be living and working in the blood, as the ego does by day. Likewise the astral body, living as it does in the whole breathing process, leaves it by night, yet the breathing goes on...

The fact is that while man lies asleep in bed, beings of the adjoining Hierarchy enter into the pulsating forces of the blood, from which the ego has departed. Angels, Archangels and Archai are then indwelling the organs in which the human ego dwells in waking life by day. Moreover in the breathing organs we have forsaken, beings of the next higher Hierarchy, Exusiai, Dynamis and Kyriotetes, are then living. Thus when we go to sleep at night, setting forth with our ego and astral body, Angels, Archangels and higher spiritual beings enter into us and animate these organs while we are outside, until we reawaken.

What is more, as to our ether body, even in waking life we are not able to fulfil what is needed there. The beings of the highest Hierarchy, Seraphim, Cherubim and Thrones, have to indwell this ether body even while we are awake; they remain there always. Lastly the physical body: if we ourselves had to achieve all the great and wonderful processes taking place there, we should not merely do it very badly; we could not set about it all. Here we are utterly helpless. What outer anatomy ascribes to the physical body could not even move a single atom of it. Powers of quite another order belong to it. These are none other than those that have been known since primaeval times as the supreme Trinity, the Powers of the Father, Son and Spirit, the essential Trinity, who indwell the physical body of man.

Therefore throughout our earthly life, our physical body is not our own. If it depended on us, it could not develop. It is, as was said of old, the true Temple of the Godhead, of the thrice-apparent Godhead... There is a constant activity within the human being proceeding not only from man himself. He only lives in this bodily nature in waking life, so to speak, as a sub-tenant. At the same time it is the Temple and dwelling place of the beings of the Hierarchies.

Bearing all this in mind, we only see the outer form of man aright if we admit: it is a picture, a picture of the working together of all the Hierarchies. They are within it... Only when things are seen in this way can one speak rightly in detail of what is commonly explained in a rather abstract manner. It is said that the physical world is not reality, it is a maya, and the reality is behind it. That is too general, as if one were to say: flowers grow in the meadow. Just as we can only do something about it if we know what kind of flowers, so knowledge of the higher world can only be put into practice if we can point out in detail *how* it works in the outer picture, maya or reflection which is its physical, sense-perceptible manifestation.

I gaze into the darkness:
In it arises light —
Living light.

Who is this light in the darkness?
I am myself in my reality.
This reality of the 'I'
Does not enter my earthly life.
I am mere picture of it.
But I shall find it again
When I am,
In good will towards the spirit,
Beyond the portal of death.

SOURCES, FURTHER READING AND PRACTICAL APPLICATIONS

The English title from which the extract is drawn is followed by the date — and, in the case of lectures, the place — of origin. The GA number identifies the volume of the German collected edition (*Gesamtausgabe*) containing the original text.

EDITOR'S FOREWORD

Further Reading: *Rudolf Steiner. An Autobiography.* S. Easton: *Herald of a New Epoch.* A. P. Shepherd: *Scientist of the Invisible.* G. Wachsmuth: *The Life and Work of Rudolf Steiner.*

CHAPTER 1 — INTRODUCTORY

1. *Knowledge of the Higher Worlds — How is it Achieved?* Ch.1, 1904. GA 10.
2. *Theosophy,* Ch. 1, 1904. GA 9.
3. *Occult Science: An Outline.* Ch. 1, 1910. GA 13.

CHAPTER 2 — THE NATURE OF MAN

1. 'At the Gates of Spiritual Science', Lec. 1. Stuttgart, 22 August 1906. GA 95.
2. 'Theosophy of the Rosicrucians', Lec. 8. Munich, 1 June 1907. GA 99.
3. 'Gospel of St John', Lec. 10. Hamburg, 30 May 1908. GA 103.
4. 'Planetary Spheres and their Influence', Lec. 3. London, 30 August 1922. GA 214.
5. 'Anthroposophy: An Introduction', Lec. 7. Dornach, 8 February 1924. GA 234.

Further Reading: Theosophy. Occult Science: An Outline. The Evolu-

tion of Consciousness. Apocalypse of St John.

CHAPTER 3 — FROM DEATH TO REBIRTH

1. 'Between Death and Rebirth', Lec. 9. Berlin, 4 March 1913. GA 141.
2. 'Planetary Spheres and their Influence', Lec. 2. Oxford, 22 August 1922. GA 214.
3. *Three Essays on Haeckel and Karma.* 1903. GA 34.
4. 'The Evolution of Consciousness', Lecs. 10 & 11. Penmaenmawr, 28/29 August 1923. GA 227.
5. 'Karmic Relationships', Vol. 8, Lec. 5. London, 24 August 1924. GA 240.

Further Reading: Theosophy. Earthly Death and Cosmic Life. Supersensible Man.

CHAPTER 4 — DESTINY AND INNER REALITY

1. *Anthroposophical Quarterly*, 1978 No 23/1. Berlin, 15 October 1906. GA 96.
2. 'Reincarnation and Karma', Lec. 3. Stuttgart, 20 February 1912. GA 135.
3. *Knowledge of the Higher Worlds — How is it Achieved?* Part II, 5. 1904. GA 10.
4. *Four Mystery Dramas: I — 'The Portal of Initiation',* Scene 2. GA 14.

Further Reading: Karmic Relationships (Vols 1 to 8).

CHAPTER 5 — EXPERIENCES OF CHRIST

1. 'The Mystery of Golgotha'. Oxford, 27 August 1922. GA 214.
2. 'The Spiritual Guidance of Man and Humanity', Lec. 1. Copenhagen, 6 June 1911. GA 15.
3. 'The Inner Aspect of the Social Question', Lec. 2. Zurich, 11 February 1919. GA 193.
4. 'The Mysteries of Light, of Space, and of the Earth', Lec. 1. Dornach, 12 December 1919. GA 194.
5. 'Love and its Meaning in the World'. Zurich, 17 December 1912. GA 143.

Further Reading: Christianity as Mystical Fact. Lecture Cycles on each of the four Gospels.

CHAPTER 6 — COMING EVENTS

1. 'Occult Science and Occult Development', Lec. 3. London, 2 May 1913. GA 152.
2. 'The Etherisation of the Blood'. Basel, 1 October 1911. GA 130.
3. 'From Jesus to Christ', Lecs 3 & 10. Carlsruhe, 7 & 14 October 1911. GA 131.
4. 'Earthly and Cosmic Man', Lec. 6. Berlin, 14 May 1912. GA 133.
5. 'The Apocalpyse of St John', Lec 7. Nuremberg, 24 June 1908. GA 104.

CHAPTER 7 — REORDERING OF SOCIETY

1. *The Threefold Commonwealth*, Foreword. 1920. GA 24.
2. *Anthroposophy and the Social Question*. 1905/6. GA 34.
3. *Anthroposophy*, 1927 Vol II No 3. 'Capital and Credit'. 1919. GA 24.
4. 'The Work of the Angels in Man's Astral Body'. Zurich, 9 October 1918. GA 182.
5. 'How Can Mankind Find the Christ Again?' Lec. 3. Dornach, 27 December 1918. GA 187.
6. Opening Lecture of the Foundation Meeting. Dornach, 24 December 1923. GA 260.

Further Reading: Towards Social Renewal. The Social Future. World Economy.

Practical Work: Centre for Social Development, Sharpthorne, West Sussex. Transform plc (Management Development), Painswick, Glos. Mercury Provident plc (Investment), Forest Row, East Grinstead, Sussex. Camphill Village Trust (Handicapped), Delrow House, Aldenham, Watford.

CHAPTER 8 — PHILOSOPHICAL FOUNDATIONS

1. *Philosophy of Freedom*, Ch. 5. 1894. GA 4.
2. *Philosophy of Freedom*, Ch. 9. 1894. GA 4.
3. 'The Psychological Foundations of Anthroposophy'. International Philosophical Congress, Bologna, 8 April 1911. GA 35.

Further Reading: Truth and Science. Riddles of Philosophy.

CHAPTER 9 — NATURAL SCIENCE AND SPIRITUAL SCIENCE

1. 'Boundaries of Natural Science', Lecs 1 & 3. Dornach 27/29 September 1920. GA 322.
2. 'Boundaries of Natural Science', Lecs 2 to 8. Dornach, 28 September/3 October 1920. GA 322.
3. *Goethe the Scientist,* Ch. 4. 1883/5. GA 1.
4. 'Art as Seen in the Light of Mystery Wisdom', Lec. 1. Dornach, 28 December 1914. GA 275.
5. 'An Outline of Anthroposophical Medical Research', Lec. 1. London, 28 August 1924. GA 319.

Further Reading: Origins of Natural Science. Agriculture. Astronomy Course. Man, Hieroglyph of the Universe. First Scientific Course (Light). *Heat Course. Fundamentals of Theraphy* (with I. Wegman). *Spiritual Science and Medicine. Curative Education.*

Practical Work: Biodynamic Agricultural Association, Clent, Stourbridge, W. Midlands. Park Attwood Therapeutic Centre, Trimpley, Bewdley, Worcs. Weleda (UK) Ltd, (Pharmaceutical Manufacturers), Heanor Rd, Ilkeston, Derby. Some 30 Home Schools and Training Centres for children and young people in need of special education and care.

CHAPTER 10 — RENEWAL OF THE ARTS

1. 'Art as Seen in the Light of Mystery Wisdom', Lec. 1. Dornach, 28 December 1914. GA 275.
2. *Goethe as Founder of a New Science of Aesthetics.* 1889, GA 30.
3. 'Ways to a New Style in Architecture'. Dornach, 17 June 1914. GA 286.
4. 'Art as Seen in the Light of Mystery Wisdom', Lec. 5. Dornach, 1 January 1915. GA 275.
5. 'Eurythmy as Visible Speech', Lec. 1. Penmaenmawr, 26 August 1923. GA 279.

Further Reading: The Arts and their Mission. Creative Speech. Speech and Drama. Four Mystery Dramas. The Inner Nature of Music. Eurythmy as Visible Music.

Practical Work: Emerson College, Forest Row, East Grinstead, Sussex. Tobias School of Art, Dunnings Rd, East Grinstead, Sussex. London School of Eurythmy, Dunnings Rd, East Grinstead, Sussex. Ringwood-Bottom School of Eurythmy, Ashley, Ringwood, Hants. London School of Speech-Formation, Dunnings Rd, East Grinstead, Sussex. Various Eurythmy Performing Groups.

CHAPTER 11 — THE PATH OF DEVELOPMENT

1. 'The Change in the Path to Supersensible Knowledge'. Dornach, 27 May 1922. GA 212.
2. 'Occult Science and Occult Development', Lec. 2. London, 1 May 1913. GA 152.
3. *Stages of Higher Knowledge.* 1905/8. GA 12.
4. *Occult Science: An Outline,* Ch. 5. 1910. GA 13.
5. 'The Evolution of Consciousness', Lec. 6. Penmaenmawr, 24 August 1923. GA 227.

Further Reading: Knowledge of the Higher Worlds: How is it Achieved? A Road to Self-Knowledge: Threshold of the Spiritual World. The Life of the Soul. Anthroposophical Leading Thoughts.

Practical Work: Anthroposophical Society in Great Britain, 35 Park Road, London — Branches and study groups.

CHAPTER 12 — IN DAILY LIFE

1. *The Education of the Child.* 1907. GA 34..
2. 'The Effects of Spiritual Develoment', Lecs. 1 & 2. The Hague, 20/21 March 1913. GA 145.
3. 'Festivals and Their Meaning: Michaelmas', Lec. 7. Berlin, 23 May 1923, GA 224.

Further Reading: A Modern Art of Education. The Essentials of Education. Soul Economy and Waldorf Education. The Kingdom of Childhood.

Practical Work: Emerson College, Forest Row, Sussex. 11 Schools for normal children, plus a dozen more developing: Steiner Schools Fellowship, c/o Michael Hall School, Forest Row, E. Sussex.

EPILOGUE

'Man as a Picture of the Living Spirit'. London, 2 September 1923. GA 228.

Nearly all of Rudolf Steiner's works in English translation are available through the publishers of this book. Please write to:

Rudolf Steiner Press
P.O. Box 955
Bristol BS99 5QN
Great Britain

Distributors in other English-language countries are:

Australia

Rudolf Steiner Book Centre
307 Sussex Street
Sydney, NSW 2000

Canada

Tri-fold Books
81 Lawton Blvd
Toronto, Ontario M4V 1Z6

New Zealand

Steinerbooks (NZ)
181 Ladies Mile
Box 11-335, Auckland 5

South Africa

Rudolf Steiner Publications SA
P.O. Box 4891
Randburg 2125

USA

Anthroposophic Press
RR4, Box 94-A1
Hudson, NY 12534

Books both in print and out of print are also available from the Library of the Anthroposophical Society in Great Britain. Please write to:

Anthroposophical Society in GB
35 Park Road
London NW1 6XT
Great Britain

Information on the practical activities in, and contact addresses for, practical activities in Great Britain are also available from the Society.

INDEX TO DEFINITIONS OF ANTHROPOSOPHICAL TERMS

INDEX TO
MEDITATIVE VERSES

German originals may be found in GA 40 (see page 201).
Further Reading: Verses and Meditations. Truth-Wrought Words.